AF248667

1984/85 Edition

PRINT CASEBOOKS 6

The Best in

ENVIRONMENTAL GRAPHICS

Written by
Susan Braybrooke

Published by
**RC Publications, Inc.
Bethesda, MD**

First published 1984 in the
United States of America
by RC Publications, Inc.
6400 Goldsboro Road
Bethesda, MD 20817

Manufactured in Hong Kong
First Printing 1984

**PRINT CASEBOOKS 6/1984-85
EDITION/THE BEST IN
ENVIRONMENTAL GRAPHICS**
Library of Congress Catalog Card
Number 75-649585
ISBN 0-915734-43-5

**PRINT CASEBOOKS 6/1984-85
EDITION**
Complete 6-Volume Set
ISBN 0-915734-40-0

RC PUBLICATIONS
President and Publisher: Howard Cadel
Vice President and Editor: Martin Fox
Art Director/Designer: Andrew P. Kner
Managing Editor: Teresa Reese
Associate Art Director: Glenn Biren
Assistant Editor: Tom Goss
Graphic Production: Natasha Perkel
Production Assistant: Susan Norr

Although they worked just as hard as any previous year's Casebook jury, the jurors this time around seemed to have an easier time of it. They were able to pick the 28 "best" projects from some 120 submissions with a minimum of contention. And, although unanimity of verdict was rare, there seemed to be general, if tacit, agreement about what they were looking for. If this year there were no intense discussions about the Casebook's role in seeking out the cutting edge—"looking for blood," as a former juror put it—what was impressive was their serious and consistent interest in finding and applauding the creative solution to the realistic problem that confronts the environmental designer in the hard world of practice.

And this is exactly what this year's Casebook is all about—creative enhancement of the experiences of clients and community in the environments that define their daily lives—the shopping center, the office, the bank, the hospital, the travel agency, the zoo—places we go to for assistance, for business, for learning or for pleasure, but which can be lifted to a surprising extent out of the mundane, the dreary and the drab by the art of graphic design.

This seems to have been a somewhat lower-key year. Indeed, is it possible that environmental graphics can become too rowdy? In several of this year's submissions, we see designers redoing comparatively recent signing programs—not because the old ones were unattractive, but because they competed too strongly with other elements of the scene, and perhaps overlooked their prime purpose—to orient and to inform—in their efforts to be

zany or dashing. As one of the jurors put it, "There has been something like graphic overkill in a number of corporate programs." So it was with not a little relief that the jury contemplated and selected the subtle corporate identity program at Levi's Plaza in San Francisco—designed by HOK and based on an enlarged reproduction of a brass blue jeans button.

Once again, the shopping center, the mall or the galleria figured largely as a field of endeavor for graphic design, and several of the winning submissions were commended for improving the existing situation. At Citicorp Center in New York, Gottschalk & Ash's dramatic red triangular entry sign structures call attention to the atrium which, although well-known to regular patrons, does not clearly announce itself at the street. In the Mazza Gallerie, the Baltimore firm of RTKL added a turn-of-the-century black-and-white tile motif to a somewhat brutalist late 1970s building to make it more appealing at the street level. In a vast new Galleria in Fort Lauderdale, The Bugdal Group's signing program, albeit comprehensive, concentrated its chief effort on getting people in and out of the parking lots, recognizing that the misery of trying to find one's way in these places deters potential shoppers, no matter how dazzling the décor once inside the mall. And at New York's Rockefeller Center, a brand new concourse signing system by Donovan & Green looks for all the world as though it were part of the original architecture.

In keeping with this year's somewhat quieter trend, many of the color palettes lean toward earth tones, particularly when harmony with the natural environment is a program requirement. William Kissiloff's

history panels for the historic Wave Hill Hudson River estate are tan with dark brown text, while the new signing at the Minnesota Zoo is essentially black-and-white against a charcoal background.

Not all this year's winners are low key, however. Two of the most inventive and colorful solutions involve vehicles—a museum/zoo bus in Portland by Scott and Cheryl McIntyre, and a people-mover at Kennedy Airport by Diane Whitebay of the Port Authority of New York and New Jersey. In both cases, small budgets in no way inhibited the effectiveness of the design. The plane mate is large and red and almost lovable; the zoo bus is provocative enough to command attention and attract riders on its own account, never mind the pleasures it is taking one to.

The jury was conscientious in recognizing successful solutions, even where the graphic style itself left them with some doubts. Pentagram's Wakefield Fortune Travel Agency in London might be questioned for the stylized illustrations on the blown-up postcard window display—but there was no doubt in the jury's minds that this was a most effective seller of package tours, more than meeting the program requirements of the client. The Macomber Farm graphics by Keith Godard of Works seemed to be a mite confusing, but they were so pleasurably involving for their users that they were willingly included in the Casebook.

One or two observations can be made from a study of the documentation supporting the submissions. Graphic designers, although recognized as essential members of the design team, are still too often hired much too late in the process. While a certain amount of deadline pressure encourages creative momentum, impossible schedules preclude the kind of detailed study on which the most enduring solutions depend. And, sadly, the encouraging trend toward post-design evaluation seems to have slipped this year. But on the plus side, designers still seem to be doing very well with small budgets, and are by and large willing to suppress their own egos in efforts to integrate their work with the architectural context.

If this was perhaps a less self-conscious year in environmental graphics, it has nevertheless allowed graphic designers to exploit the new pluralism—freed from the shackles of polemics—to get on with the job and search for the most appropriate solution for the problem in hand. They have been able to stop worrying about whether modernism is alive, dead or dying, if high-tech or ornament are evil, and if Helvetica is passé. Interestingly, Helvetica has made quite a comeback, appearing in a very large number of this year's submissions, and no longer needing the apologia of its legibility or availability. It is simply an excellent and versatile typeface and is obviously here to stay.
—*Susan Braybrooke*

Casebook Jurors

Thomas H. Geismar

Thomas H. Geismar, as a partner in Chermayeff & Geismar Associates, the firm he founded in 1960 with Ivan Chermayeff, has been responsible for the design of over 100 corporate identification programs, including those for Xerox, Chase Manhattan Bank, and Mobil Oil. He also developed major U.S. government exhibits at Expo '67 in Montreal and Expo '70 in Osaka, as well as—in New York—the Hall of the Sun at the Hayden Planetarium and The Mill at Burlington House. Under his leadership as chairman of an advisory committee to the U.S. Department of Transportation, a new national system of standardized symbol signs was developed. In 1979, with Chermayeff, Geismar received the gold medal, highest award of the American Institute of Graphic Arts.

Nancye L. Green

A partner with Michael Donovan in the New York design firm of Donovan and Green since 1974, Nancye Green is involved in a variety of media ranging from environmental and exhibit design to advertising and print graphics to computer-driven multi-image presentations, film and video. She graduated *cum laude* from Tulane University in 1968 with a degree in urban studies. After a stint with Time Inc., she attended Parsons School of Design, graduating with honors in environmental design in 1973. Her work has included numerous advocacy planning projects under funding from the National Endowment for the Arts, H.E.W., the Ford Foundation, and others. As an art director and media producer, she has produced and staged events, presentations and meetings around the world.

Wayne Kosterman

President of Wayne Kosterman Associates since 1979 and a principal in Generic Sign Systems since 1980, Wayne Kosterman spent two years in architecture before receiving his B.S. in visual design at the Institute of Design, Chicago. Prior to starting his own companies, he served as director of environmental communications for RVI Corporation and as a designer for several other Chicago firms. Kosterman served as director and treasurer of the Society of Typographic Arts and helped found the Society of Environmental Graphic Designers. He also taught visual problem-solving at the Chicago Academy of Fine arts. Client work includes corporate identity programs and sign systems for banks, hospitals and universities.

Stuart Ash

Stuart Ash studied graphic design at Canada's Western Technical School and then, from 1962-64, at the Ontario College of Art (where he taught advanced typography in 1979). After working for Cooper and Beatty and for Paul Arthur Associates, he formed a partnership with Fritz Gottschalk which, as Gottschalk & Ash International, established offices in Montreal, Toronto, New York and Zurich. Exhibitions of the firm's work were held at the Mead Library of Ideas in New York in 1967, at the National Gallery of Canada in 1969, the Museum of Fine Arts in Montreal in 1970 and as part of a Swiss graphics exhibition at the Louvre in Paris in 1971.

Anthony Russell

Born and educated in London, Anthony Russell arrived in New York in 1963, where he established a multi-disciplined design office servicing a wide range of clients that includes Manufacturers Hanover Corporation, Corning Glass Center, Peat Marwick, New York State Urban Development Corporation and the City of New Rochelle. Russell's design studio produces annual reports, posters, catalogs, magazines and environmental graphics. The firm has a particular interest in the work for development corporations undertaking revitalization programs in downtown areas. Aside from New Rochelle, recent projects include "La Margueta" at 116th Street in Manhattan, a section of downtown Brooklyn, and the village of Nyack, New York.

Susan Braybrooke

Susan Braybrooke is a writer, editor and public relations consultant in architecture and design. She is currently working on a book on the design of research laboratories, for which she received funding from the National Endowment for the Arts. She edited the *AIA Metric Building and Construction Guide*, published by John Wiley in 1980, as well as Hugh Stubbins' book, *Architecture: The Design Experience*, which Wiley published in 1976. She was the author of *Casebooks 3, 4 and 5/ The Best in Environmental Graphics* and has published articles in a number of professional journals.

Index Projects

Farm Credit Banks

A corporate signing program for a new high-rise building in downtown Spokane, Washington, posed the problems of twin circulation systems and separate, but related, identities for three autonomous banks under the overall Farm Credit Banks umbrella. While there is not much actual day-to-day contact with the public within these banks, they are a strong financial and political force in the community, and were therefore concerned to project a sophisticated public image. Says designer Robert Bailey, "The client specifically requested a design that was elegant in a very quiet way, with no pretensions or trendiness about it."

This being so, the Robert Bailey Design Group strove to create a common graphic thread throughout all three banks, which would somehow achieve a traditional or classical feeling within an essentially slick, hi-tech setting. Since the building is aluminum-clad, a machine-like esthetic seemed appropriate for the signing, with all the graphic elements rendered in chrome-plated brass. Transparent or reflective surfaces give a light touch to a complex program that demanded individual identification for some 400 employees, as well as signing for all the building services and operational departments.

For the major building identification, 9″ by 2″ (deep) chrome-plated brass letters in Berling type were mounted on the aluminum building skin. Once inside the lobby, the first things you see are the directories—triangular, gray glass monoliths (mounted on polished black granite bases) with illuminated graphics on three sides—something that was technically quite difficult to accomplish. Entries to the bank floors are highlighted by means of numbered glass panels striped with white gold leaf. Each bank is identified by its name in 4″ by ⅜″ chrome-plated brass lettering mounted on a fabric wall in the reception area. In an unusual touch, conference room identification employs thin, cut-out chrome-plated brass dimensional letters applied to glass that has been sandblasted in stripes.

At the level of the individual employees, two types of chrome-plated brass signs are used—wall-mounted or desk modules. These are photomechanically etched with the bank's name, and receive movable acrylic name inserts for the individual employee, printed subsurface in Helvetica Medium with the background color matching the color code for the bank. Burgundy, dark green and tan are the colors of the respective banks. Bank presidents reveal their status by virtue of solid brass chrome-plated desk modules with their

2.

3.

1.

4.

5.

6.

7.

1. Seventeen-story, aluminum-clad building houses three separate banks needing distinct but related graphic identity.
2. Chrome-plated brass letters in Berling type are mounted on the side of the building to establish its identity in the cityscape.
3. Similar lettering is used inside lobby to mark double circulation system. Directories are illuminated gray glass monoliths on polished granite bases.
4. Thin, cut-out letters applied to striped glass walls identify conference rooms.
5. White gold-leaf numbers and stripes announce individual bank's floors.
6. Transparency is achieved by reflective surfaces and listing of component departments directly on glass wall.
7. Basic signing for departments and individuals employs a system of wall-mounted milled brass frames with acrylic inserts and Helvetica type.

own and the bank's names photomechanically etched.

There was considerable refinement of the system as it evolved to meet the client's demand for simplicity, clarity and elegance. Some problems arose because both chrome-plating and etching are two processes that inevitably produce a fairly high percentage of letters that have to be redone. But close cooperation with a competent sign company kept the momentum going despite this relatively high reject rate. The Casebook jury felt that this was a particularly successful corporate program—one which managed to be clear and coherent throughout the entire sign hierarchy, while remaining understated. "I've seen many of these kinds of comprehensive corporate program," said one juror, "but not many are this well done at every level."

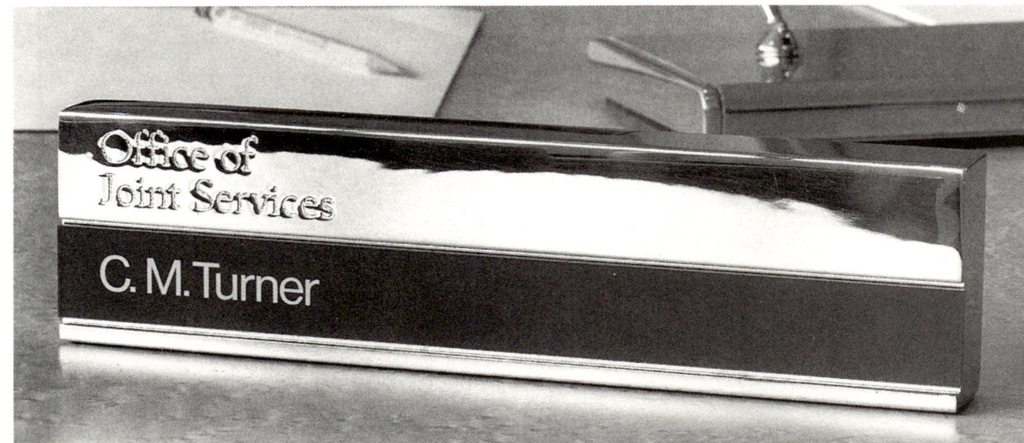

8.

9.

8-10. Individual signs for some 400 employees are either wall-mounted or desk modules. Each includes photomechanically etched name of component bank and movable acrylic insert identifying employee. Bank presidents have solid brass desk modules with all lettering photo-etched.
11. Floor plan showing placement of signs.
12. Individual banks and special departments are identified by cut-out chrome-plated brass letters applied to fabric-covered walls.
13, 14. Changeable letterboards in cafeteria employ Helvetica Medium for a change of mood.

10.

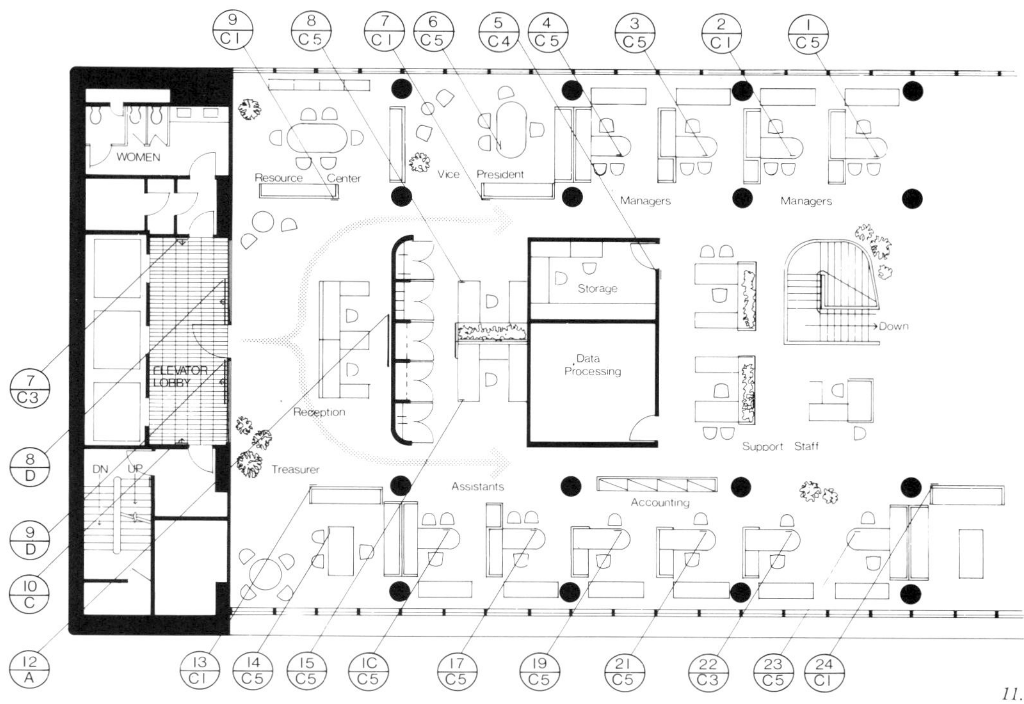

11.

Client: Farm Credit Banks of Spokane, Washington

Design firm: Robert Bailey Design Group, Portland, OR

Designers: Robert L. Bailey, design partner; Dale Hoover, senior designer; Joseph Readdy, technical manager; Paul Besserman, associate designer; Carolyn Coghlan, colorist/graphics

Architect: Walker, McGough, Foltz, Lyerla, PS; Bruce M. Walker, principal-in-charge; Gerald P. Adkins, director of design

Interior designer: Zimmer, Gunsul, Frasca Partnership; John A. Walling, director of design; John A. Moll, project manager

Fabricators: Architectural Signing, Inc. (prime contractor); Architectural Signing Northwest, Inc.; Environmental Signing, Inc. (subcontractor, individual letter fabrication)

12.

13.

14.

Levi's Plaza

Although an elaborate exterior signing system—replete with directories, directional signs and banners—was originally considered for this four-building, four-block corporate headquarters in San Francisco, the ultimate decision was for understated elegance and minimal signing that would let the architecture read through, and the client's chief product speak for itself.

Since Levi Strauss is the major tenant—occupying three out of the four buildings—the symbol of a blue jeans button was adopted, magnified and most elegantly executed in brass against a chrome-plated brass background. The mirror motif was chosen as a device for reflecting the architecture of the buildings, and the handsomely landscaped plaza they surround, as well as to emphasize the ornamental metal at building entries. The chrome plaques are in turn floated on large, glass panels beside the doors, except in one case where the plaque is mounted on brick.

The building names, set in Clarendon type, are photo-etched into the chrome background and enamel-filled—the blue of the enamel recalling the blue denim of which jeans are made. The buttons, 7¾″ in diameter, are mechanically fastened to the 20⅛″ square chrome panels.

Even though there is some additional signing identifying such features as the fountain in the plaza, this is kept to a minimum. The jury felt that, in this case, the appropriateness of the building plaques, the care with which they are executed, and the richness of the materials do as much as, if not more than, an elaborate multi-faceted and multi-colored scheme to identify and promote the good name of the client corporation.

Client: Levi Strauss (San Francisco)
Design firm: Hellmuth, Obata & Kassabaum, Inc., St. Louis, MO
Designers: Charles P. Reay, director of graphic design; Greg Youngstrom, project designer
Architect: Hellmuth, Obata & Kassabaum (San Francisco); Gyo Obata, director of design; Bill Valentine, project designer

1.

1. *Magnified brass jeans button becomes Levi Strauss corporate headquarters symbol.*
2, 5. *Beautifully landscaped site is reflected in brass, chrome and glass signing vocabulary.*
3, 4. *Brass symbols are mounted on chrome-plated brass backgrounds which reflect site and architecture. Plaques are floated on glass in three out of four buildings, but in one is case-mounted directly on brick.*

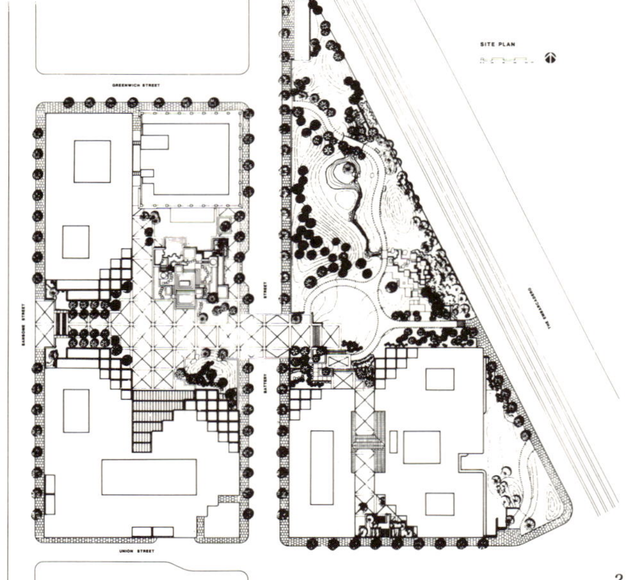

2.

LEVI STRAUSS & CO
S.F. CAL
Levi Strauss
Building

LEVI STRAUSS & CO
S.F. CAL
Stern
Building

3.

4.

5.

The design of history panels and a series of ground markers for the 28-acre Wave Hill estate on the Hudson River involved the graphic designers in the study of the history of the place, the collation and organization of vast amounts of documentary material, the use of a fabrication system that would withstand the elements, and an overall concept of the graphics program as something that would enhance a beautiful natural setting by pointing out interesting features, but in a very low-key voice.

Wave Hill is the only Hudson River estate in New York City preserved for the public. It uses its historic buildings and gardens for cultural programs related to the themes of man and nature and the interaction between them. The graphics program was seen as an introduction to the cultural resources of the place, which must be sensitive to its visual and spiritual character.

When designer William Kissiloff became involved, his initial role was to help the institution prepare an application to the National Endowment for the Humanities to fund this historical interpretive program, which he then went on to implement graphically. The central concept is a series of six panels—displayed on a terrace within the grounds—which together depict the chronological history of Wave Hill from the 17th century when the land was given by the Dutch to one Adriaen Van der Dock, to the 1840s when the house was built by the New York attorney William Morris, to its development as a planned villa

Welcome to Wave Hill

You are invited to enjoy Wave Hill—the grounds and gardens, the greenhouses and the public facilities of Wave Hill House itself. And you are especially encouraged to experience the great panoramic view of one of nature's geologic wonders—the Palisades, framed by the Hudson River. Before you commence your visit, we suggest you spend at least a few minutes acquainting yourself with the Wave Hill Historic Interpretive Exhibit. It tells the story of how this unique man-made environment came into being over the last century and a half, and how it has influenced social, political and aesthetic values in the world beyond its fieldstone boundary walls. Do enjoy Wave Hill, and please respect these few rules.

"It is a scientific fact that the occasional contemplation of natural scenes of an impressive character...in connection with relief from ordinary cares, changes of air and changes of habits, is favorable to the health and vigor of men, and to their intellect."

Frederick Law Olmsted
1865

No: bikes, pets, chairs, blankets, radios, sports, picnicking, littering, picking of flowers, or climbing.

1.

Wave Hill Site Map

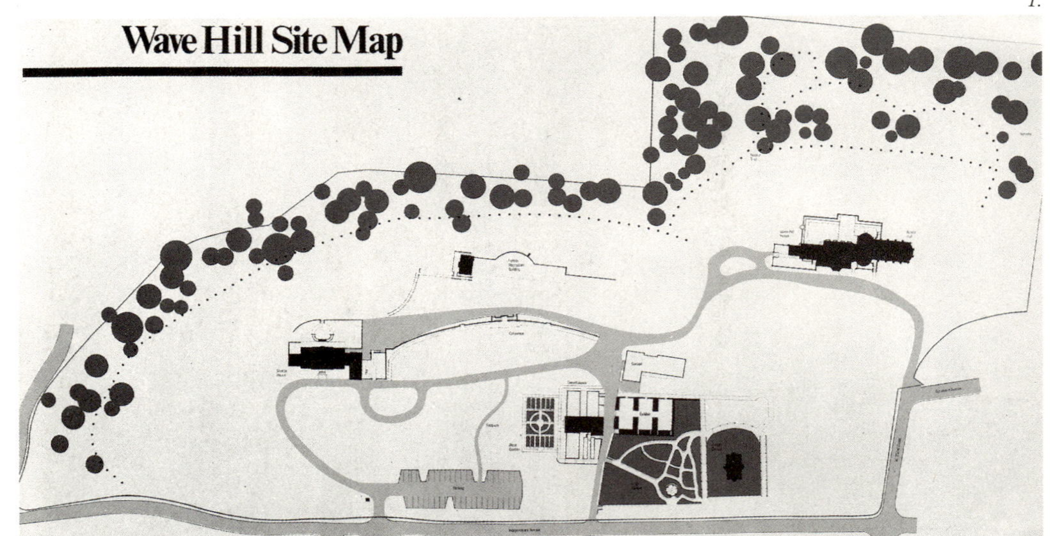

2.

Aquatic Garden

Under-surface of *Victoria* leaf. Engraving by E.W. Smith.

Early photographs suggest that this garden—popularly a "lily pond"—was probably created by the Perkins family's head gardener, Albert Millard, between 1915-26. The garden's main attraction now is the giant Victoria lily (Victoria amazonia). Called "the vegetable wonder of the Victorian world," this plant's circular tray-like leaf commonly reaches a diameter of four feet and sometimes as much as six feet. The largest leaves are capable of supporting a small child in raft-like suspension.

The Victoria lily was discovered in the Amazon by English explorers in 1833, and it promptly created a horticultural sensation. Sir Joseph Paxton, the great 19th Century planner and designer, credited the structural pattern of the plant (see left) as the inspiration for the form of a glass conservatory to house the plant and later for his architectural masterpiece, the Crystal Palace in London.

3.

4.

1. *Entrance welcome sign sets low-key, picturesque tone of graphic program.*
2. *Graphic site plan introduces visitors to cultural resources of buildings and grounds.*
3. *Ground markers describing individual components contain carefully compressed historical texts that demanded considerable scholarly research.*
4. *Six history panels mounted in the garden trace the story of the mansion and its grounds from the 17th century to the present day.*

5.

6.

community and the residence of both Mark Twain and Theodore Roosevelt, to 1960 when the estate was donated to New York City. In addition to these "timeline" panels, Kissiloff also designed an area site plan, an entrance welcome sign, and ground markers identifying and describing trees and plant species and the different greenhouse and garden collections.

The Modulite process for fiberglass embedment of the graphics was used to create a solid graphic unit that can never delaminate or peel apart. By this process, graphics are silkscreened onto specially developed carrier sheets, using inks that have been developed to permanently retain their initial color brilliancy. The sheets are then saturated with polyester resin and permanently embedded between tightly-woven fiberglass cloth reinforced layers, which are finally baked and cured. All hardware—supports and trim—are anodized aluminum (with concrete footings). Times Bold was specified for all heading type, Times Roman for general copy and captions, and Univers 77 for notations. Panel backgrounds are tan with dark brown text and muted colors and earthtones for the graphics. The result is extremely harmonious with the natural environment.

The images used were selected with enormous care from a vast archive of varied printed and photographic materials, and Kissiloff worked throughout this process in close collaboration with a team of distinguished scholars.

5, 6. History panels containing carefully researched text and illustrations have been fabricated using a fiberglass embedment technique to create a solid graphic unit that is impervious to weather.

Client: Wave Hill, Inc. (Riverdale, New York City); Betty Greenfield, executive director; Nora Mandell, project planning; Marco Polo Stufano, director of horticulture; Ellen de Nooyer, research; Mark Belmuth, program coordination
Design firm: Kissiloff Associates, Inc., New York City
Designers: William Kissiloff, project design director; Don Kline, graphic designer; Philip Welle, structural detailing; Peter Brill, mechanical art
Fabricators: Warren Displays (construction installation); Pannier Corp. (graphic lamination)
Consultants: Dr. Albert Fine (historical research); William Houseman (text); Milo Stewart (interpretive planner); Nancy Cole, Dr. Thomas Elia (horticultural historians); Dr. Richard Chamatz (geological history); Dr. Stephen Stertz (research)

Construction Barricades

The positive public relations value of an attractive construction barricade is becoming quite well documented. Not only does it alert prospective tenants to available office or retail space, but it prepares the public for a new presence in the cityscape. If people enjoy the graphics on the barricade, then they are probably predisposed to like the building, too. The jurors chose three barricades—one each in New York, Chicago and Los Angeles—for inclusion in this Casebook.

525 West Monroe Street

Chermayeff & Geismar's design for the barricade at 525 West Monroe Street in Chicago, a high-rise building designed by Skidmore, Owings & Merrill, was bold enough to be seen from a considerable distance. The number "525" in Helvetica Bold was painted white against a bright red field on a series of 12′-high plywood fins attached to a curved span above the primary entrance to the site. "The curving form, combined with the fin treatment," say the designers, "allowed the bold display to be read from Wacker Drive and other major intersections blocks away from the site. The 525 was readable from an arc of 180 degrees, yet appeared different from every angle, and continually changed as one moved past it. The curved form also reflected the shape and location of the future building entrance." The remainder of the barricade was low-key by contrast, consisting of a 6′ gray band above a 4′ dark blue band, with a thin red line separating the two. Studies of the site, traffic flow, and

1.

2.

3.

1. Sample of fin structure with numeral at one-sixth of actual size.
2. Scale model of "525"—essential in determining size and legibility within the surrounding cityscape.
3. Actual barricade sign can be read from an arc of 180 degrees.

Client: Tishman Speyer Properties (Chicago); Robert Belcaster
Design firm: Chermayeff & Geismar Associates, New York City
Designers: Tom Geismar, Julia Bredbenner
Fabricator: Arrow Sign Co.

building colors influenced the height of the fence, its curved configuration and the color palette. An initial idea to have the numerals free-standing atop the fence was too expensive and would not have provided the visual interest of the final scheme.

520 Madison Avenue
Now that construction barricades have become a vibrant form of street art, we miss them when they are gone. Without them, the unfinished building looks messy at street level, and the empty storefronts a depressing void in the streetscape. To counteract this problem at their new building at 520 Madison Avenue, New York, Tishman Speyer Properties commissioned designers Chermayeff & Geismar to replace the barrier which they had designed (see

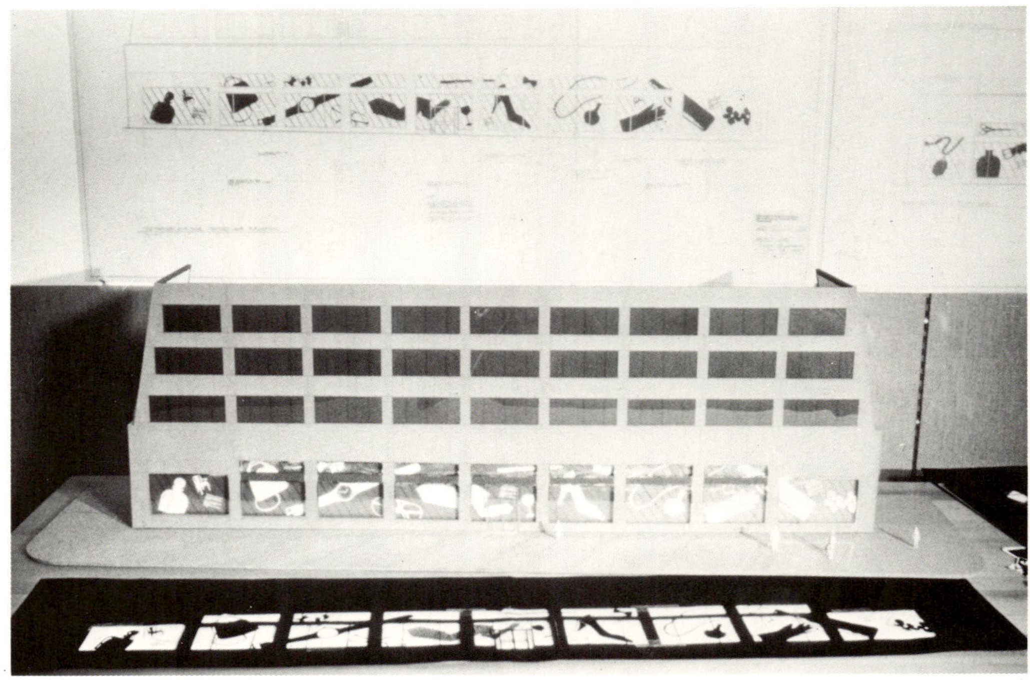

4.

5.

Environmental Graphics Casebook 5, pages 40-41) with a series of panels to go behind the glass and call attention to the retail potential for appropriate tenants.

With three months to complete the assignment, the designers studied the window locations and construction, as well as angles of view from Madison Avenue. They then

6.

developed a series of preliminary sketches, which were translated into models for presentation to the client. The final design consisted of large-scale graphic renditions of the kinds of objects suitable tenants might sell—from watches to gloves to bottles of wine—which appeared to float across a series of single-colored backgrounds overlaid with a red diagonal pinstripe.

The design was painted onto very large ¼″ masonite panels, invisibly joined, which were attached to the inner window mullions so as to directly abut the glass. The objects were white; background colors were bright orange, purple and brown latex paint; pinstripes were vinyl tape. Necessary rental information in Univers 77 type was silkscreened in white directly onto the window glass.

Other design alternatives were considered at the beginning—such as trompe-l'oeil views of construction workers, or of pedestrians peering into the building from the sidewalk, but these were rejected because they told one nothing about the space available, and also because the windows were not exactly at street level, which would destroy the illusion. The executed scheme has been successful enough to generate calls to the designers from other building owners interested in doing the same kind of thing themselves.

Crocker Center

The developer of an important 44-54-story commercial center under construction in downtown Los Angeles wanted to use the construction barricade to call

7.

4-6. Preliminary sketches and a scale model were necessary to determine the impact and convince the client of the effectiveness of this bold scheme for storefront panels to replace the construction barricade.

7, 8. Stylized renditions of potential retail wares floating across a series of single-colored backgrounds introduce drama to the streetscape and attract potential store tenants.

Client: Tishman Speyer Properties (New York City)
Design firm: Chermayeff & Geismar Associates, New York City
Designer: Tom Geismar
Fabricator: Mack Sign Co.

8.

attention to the project, its architecture, and the people and companies associated with it. Responding to this, the design firm of Hinsche + Associates devised a series of plywood panels, cut out in geometric shapes, through which scaffolding and interior plywood walls—painted in bold red, blue, orange and yellow— would gleam cheerfully out in the predominantly gray streetscape. The color changes on interior walls and scaffolding occurred at points where these disappeared behind the solid parts of the cut-outs. The cut plywood panels were painted gray, with the words "Crocker Center"—4' high—reversed out in white. Thirty-foot-high, geometrically cut panels, also painted gray, which reflected the architectural forms of the Crocker Center buildings, were erected at corners of the barricade, bearing in white the names of the major people and companies associated with Crocker Center. The subcontractors' names were painted in white on the gray exterior panels of the barricade. Helvetica Medium and Bold was used throughout in letter sizes ranging from 3" to 10" high.

Since the barricade encompassed the entire 4-acre site, the graphics were deliberately made bold enough to be seen by people within a three- or four-block radius of the Center, and the corner panels read from 50' to 60' away.

Hinsche + Associates got involved four months after construction had begun and a partial barricade had already been erected. With a $12,000 design budget and a two-month schedule, they set to work conducting a careful survey of pedestrian and vehicular traffic on the surrounding blocks and taking numerous photos to establish scale and environmental character. They developed construction drawings, and coordinated all their work with the architects.

One problem did occur with the fabrication of the corner panels: their weight and size demanded considerable structural strength to withstand the forces of wind and their own weight. In the end, the panels were supported from behind by steel I beams.

The jury liked the bold, simple concept, which they felt worked well in the complex and often rather drab environment of downtown Los Angeles.

Client: Maguire Partners (Santa Monica, CA)
Design firm: Hinsche + Associates, Santa Monica, CA
Design firm: Hinsche + Associates, Santa Monica, CA
Architect: Jim Lim, Beck/Turner Construction
Fabricator: J.P. Carroll Co. (painting)
Consultant: CHT Sign Painters, Inc.

9.

10.

11.

12.

13.

9-13. *Geometrically-cut plywood panels, evolved in model form and then translated to the streetscape, announce a new building by reflecting its architectural forms. Bold, 4'-high Helvetica letters announce the name of the project to people within a three or four block radius.*

The new City Hall in Hull, Quebec, is much more than the traditional civic complex. It contains an interior plaza or agora, a library, a community center with several meeting rooms, a festival hall, a sports center, and several floors of office space. When the designers, GSM, were retained to create a signing system for the building, a signature was needed, as well as directional and informational graphics to communicate its purposes and resources to the community. Hired at a very early stage in the project, when the architects were still in the conceptual design phase, GSM conducted preliminary studies in close collaboration with the architects so that, as far as possible, signing and lighting could be integrated with each other and unified with the architecture.

Inspired by the architecture, GSM created an essential three-dimensional system, in which handsome, free-standing or wall-mounted baked enamel metal sign structures support simple, stylized messages in condensed Helvetica type. The condensed Helvetica face distinguishes City Hall from the neighboring government complex, where Helvetica Regular is used. It also fits well into the vertical rectangular sign fields. The symbol, the related arrow, and the pictograms were evolved to suggest the components and forms of the architecture, as well as the open, two-way communication between City Hall and the community. Executed in burnt umber/ orange tones on a white background with black type, the signs complement but do not

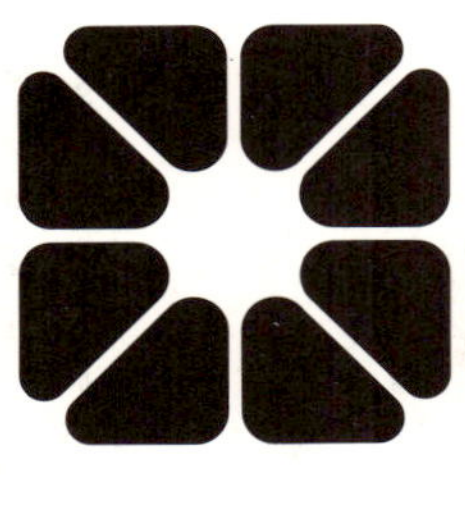

Maison du Citoyen Hull

1.

2.

1, 2. Logo and pictograms, as well as directional arrow, used in conjunction with condensed Helvetica type, were devised by the designers to express the architecture of the complex and emphasize direct communication between city government and community.
3. Brick buildings surround dramatic, glass-walled agora or interior plaza.

3.

4.

6.   7.

4. *Most outdoor signs have white type on an orange background. Pictograms are rendered simply in dark brown/black.*

5, 7. *Inside, directional signs are burnt umber/orange on white with black type, essentially reversing the exterior color palette.*

6. *Subtle color palette is differently combined in the main building identification sign, where white lettering and brown background are enlivened by green arrow background and orange logo.*

clash with the rich brick hues of the building's walls. Smaller signs have an olive background, and some cut letters are applied directly to architectural surfaces. Outdoor signs have white type on a dark background.

The fact that the final scheme remains close to the initial concept says much for the pertinacity of the designers, who managed to maintain a responsive working relationship with the architects during a lengthy project development period and a change in architectural team leadership. It also demanded close supervision of the fabrication and installation efforts to ensure a high level of detailing and careful integration with the architectural finishes.

8. Condensed type is particularly effective on monolith identifying the agora.
9, 10, 11, 13. Arrow and pictograms were developed along with the basic logo/symbol to symbolize the architecture and the democratic intentions of the complex.
12, 14, 15. Hardware—essentially free-standing, ceiling-hung, or wall-mounted baked-enamel sign structures—was selected to complement the architecture.

8.

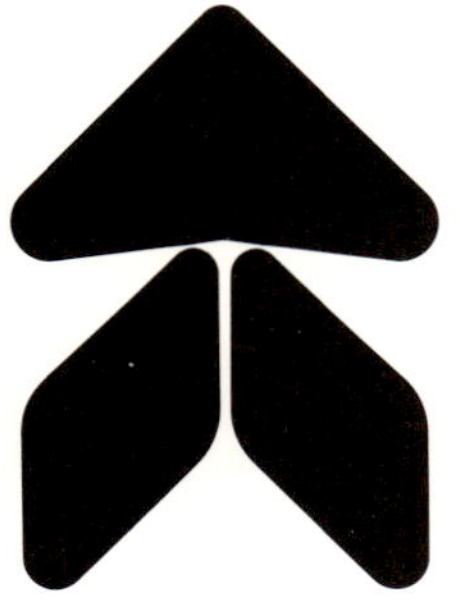

9.

10.

11.

12.

13.

Client: City of Hull, Maison du Citoyen
(Quebec)
Design firm: GSM Design, Inc.,
Montreal, Quebec
Architect: Lazosky & Cayer
Fabricator: Simpson's Contract
Division

14.

15.

If the art of environmental graphics did much to enliven the banality of the typical shopping center of the 1960s, the skill of the graphic designer is now being called upon to chart a rational course through the welter of experiences that threaten to overwhelm one in the malls, galleries and atria of the 1980s. The charge to The Bugdal Group, when they undertook environmental graphics for the Galleria in Fort Lauderdale, Florida, was something of this kind. They were asked to unify the different elements in a large, fractured complex and to pay particular attention to clarifying the site access and parking arrangements which extended over four separate garages and several surface lots. The problem was complicated by state zoning restrictions, which made it difficult to give vehicular access signs the position and scale they needed for complete clarity. But this was partially solved by placing most of the signs on county easements, where such restrictions are not in force.

Because the designers were not hired until construction of the complex was half-finished, they had to produce a temporary signing system. But this worked out to everyone's advantage, as it could be used to test public response to sign messages and locations, as well as the effectiveness of the proposed color-coding system, before decisions were frozen. Based on these responses, final scale mockups were constructed for presentation to the client before bid documents were completed. In order to start fabrication as soon as

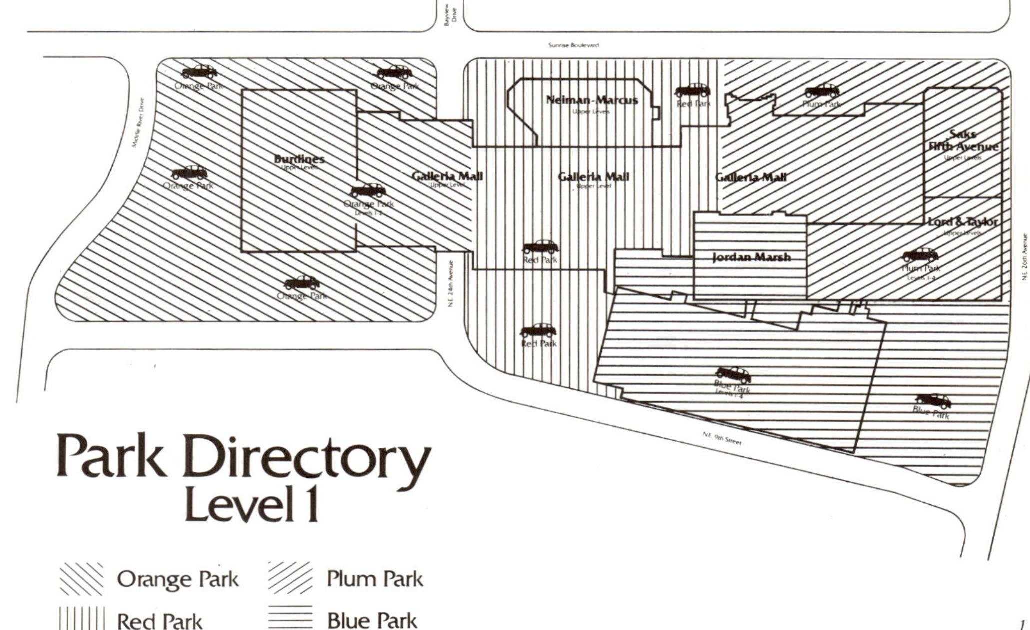

Park Directory
Level 1

1.

2.

possible, implementation was undertaken in three phases—working from the outside in. Parking garage signing and perimeter roadways and parking lots constituted the first two phases, followed by entry and mall interior signs.

A color-coding palette of orange, red, blue and plum is used on main parking and shopping area signs, identifying each in relation to the major department stores. Inside the garages, overhead signs direct vehicular traffic flow; and throughout the parking areas, a system of colors, numbers and letters of the alphabet define levels, sections and rows so that it becomes virtually impossible to forget where you left your car. Color-coded cast letters, attached to the exterior walls of the building, direct people into the parking areas and thence to the Galleria entrances where they can find vertical transportation to take them up to the mall. Vertical transition lobbies are painted in the basic color code to attract shoppers to the mall entrances. Here, too, there are directories giving detailed information as to relative location in relation to major stores. Inside the mall are additional directories and pylon markers to identify the individual stores and direct shoppers back to their cars again.

The main entrance to the Galleria is highlighted by an elegant, 12′-diameter gold-painted aluminum disc with reverse-channel illuminated letters. At night, a radiant glow is achieved by means of the diffused reflection of yellow neon against the gold metallic background. Most of the other signs are of aluminum construction with polyurethane paint finishes and vinyl die-cut texts. The metallic effect on the main sign is achieved by the use of gold automotive paint. Fritz Quadrata type is used throughout because it conforms well with existing type styles and has a certain casual elegance about it.

The Casebook jury thought that shoppers in the Galleria certainly ought to be grateful for the very detailed attention given to directing them in and out of the parking areas. For these large amorphous spaces are often quite bewildering, giving one the feeling that, once inside, one may never emerge again.

3.

1, 2. Color-coding and accessible directories within parking areas and at transitional points between parking and mall do much to clarify an essentially complex parking situation.
3. Sketch for Galleria wall graphics.
4. Main entrance identification is a 12′-diameter, gold-painted aluminum disc which glows at night.

4.

5.

7.

8.

9.

5. Cast letters painted to conform with color-coding system identify entrances to Galleria and parking.
6. Column-mounted parking garage identification includes color code, level and row.
7, 8. Curbside directional signs are color-coded to relate to major stores. Message strips can be changed without use of exposed screws or fasteners, as access is via removable top cap.
9. Plaza parking signs are lamppost-mounted with top and bottom panels to conceal mounting hardware.

Client: Leonard L. Farber Co. (Pompano Beach, FL)
Design firm: The Bugdal Group, Coral Gables, FL
Designers: Dick Bugdal and Margaret Montgomery, principal designers; Elsa Lopez, project manager
Fabricators: Melweb Signs; Colite Industries; Acolite Sign Co.

Wakefield Fortune Travel

A respected and successful British travel agency, Wakefield Fortune nonetheless tended to evoke an aura of elderly clerks in musty offices seeking out impeccable pensions for maiden ladies, or making high-level but discreet travel arrangements for the corporate élite. In fact, Wakefield Fortune is a with-it, albeit established, organization catering to a wide public and committed to a personal approach to each of its clients. Recognizing the need for a radical overhaul of its corporate image, Wakefield Fortune hired Pentagram to create a wholly new identity for the agency, which would express the global and democratic reality of its philosophy and performance.

Although the design program embraced everything from work stations to luggage tags, the chief focus of the effort was a series of high-street store fronts, which now offer the casual passerby an unequivocal invitation to see the world. The first step in the redesign program was to extend the agency's name from Wakefield Fortune to Wakefield Fortune Travel and to create a three-dimensional logo, which is mounted in bold sculptural silver letters against a blue fascia band above the shop window. The shadow line of the letters takes up the 45-degree angle of the fascia and establishes a dramatic presence that shines out among the run-of-the-mill shops on a typical English high street on a typical drab day. The major display element is a concertina or zig-zag of giant postcards (ten times normal size) bearing evocative images of the Wakefield Fortune services and

1.

2.

realistic written messages. Enclosed in their own reinforced glass box, the postcards project beyond the storefront itself and angle up to become part of the fascia.

Inside the store, two areas are demarcated by design—a blue-tiled instant-information area with gondolas full of .brochures, and a red-carpeted platform with comfortable seats and a specially designed counter, across which prospective travelers can consult with the individual agents in a direct and informal way. Each agent is identified by means of a small version of the postcard zig-zag. The 3D logotype is applied to particularly good effect on the jazzy little mini-cars which buzz about all day delivering tickets and documents to clients' homes and offices.

The program was designed, developed, and a prototype store constructed within a five-month period. Building of the prototype store at Twickenham, on the fringe of the Greater London area, was compressed into an eight-week schedule, during which it was "business as usual" for the agency. The fascia bands were made from painted alucabond aluminum panels, selected because they could be formed to a 45-degree angle without rippling. Aluminum angle frame and glass complete the storefront. Designed to meet the demands of the projecting fascia and postcard zig-zag, the special 3D typeface was used thoughout on all screened or printed applications. White, blue and primary red are the dominant interior colors, but there is a good deal of yellow in the

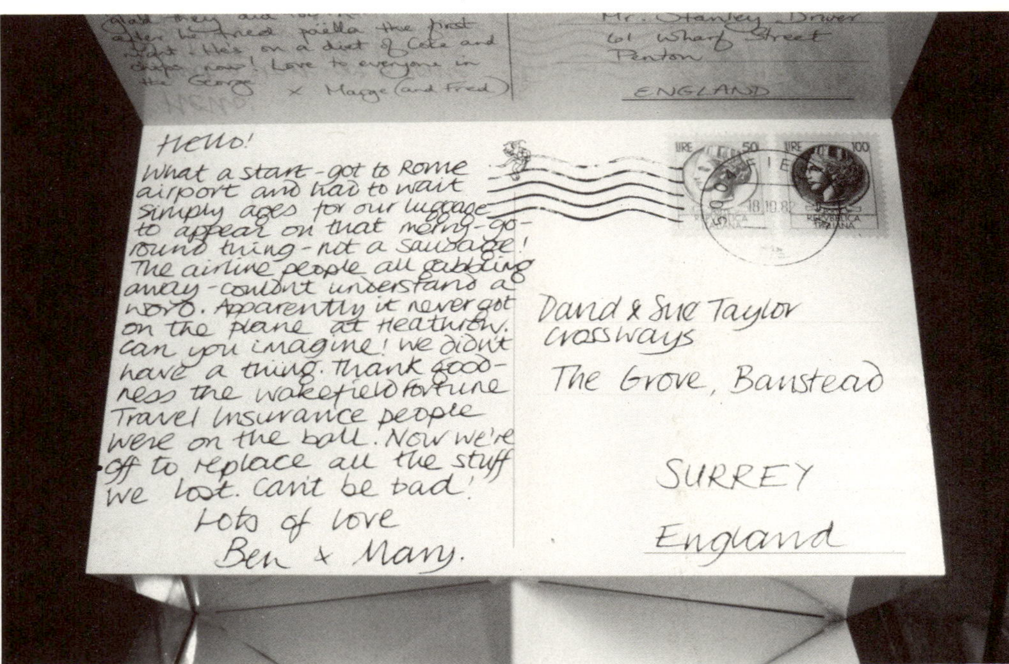

3.

4.

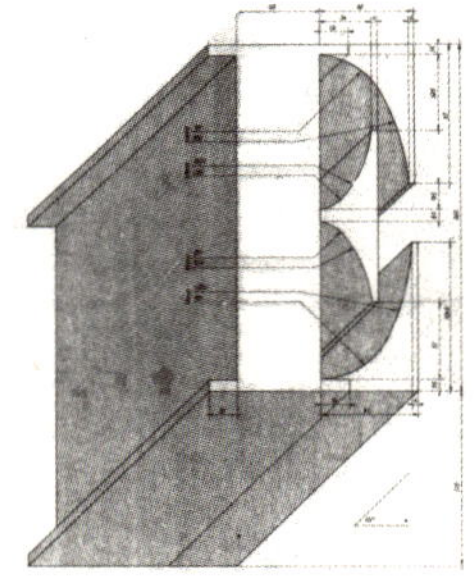

5.

illustrations to denote sun and sand.

Few changes were made during design development. The client and apparently the local approval authority were taken with the wit and originality of the postcard idea, as was the Casebook jury. Some jurors had a question about the graphic style, but all applauded the scheme's ability to evoke the lure of travel and make one want to take a trip.

3. Blown-up postcards have realistic messages.
4. Specially designed "gondolas" display a welter of brochures inside the store.
5. Shop drawing of the letter "E".
6-9. Postcard illustrations are stylized renditions of Wakefield Fortune's chief travel and tour services. They are displayed in a reinforced glass box that projects beyond the storefront window.

Client: Wakefield Fortune Travel (Cheam, Surrey, England)
Design firm: Pentagram Design Ltd., London
Illustrator: Bob Norrington
Fabricators: Griffin Shopfitters; Carter Design Group (brochure racks and millwork)

Talleyrand Office Park

Office parks are viewed by many as the workplaces of the future—not to mention the present—and so competition among them is keen. Developers are finding that a well-planned environment is an excellent sales tool, and they are anxious to communicate the high quality of their office complex to prospective tenants as directly and distinctively as possible. With this in mind, the Robert Martin Company hired designers Gottschalk + Ash to create a sculptural sign for the Talleyrand Office Park in Tarrytown, New York. With only eight weeks to complete the work, and while access roadways were still under construction, the designers surveyed vantage points from roads approaching and passing the site to ensure that the sign would be equally visible to oncoming traffic in two directions, and its message— the name and address of the park—legible from some distance. The sign they arrived at is a sculptural assemblage of eight 8'-high aluminum "T's" (for Talleyrand), placed one behind the other in a parallelogram-shaped configuration. Each T was painted a different shade in a color gradation of green to blue. The siting of the T's is perpendicular to the main thoroughfare so that the end T's bearing the name of the office park are visible from either direction. Because of the parallelogram configuration, the eastbound driver sees the color gradation from green to blue, while the westbound rider experiences it from blue to green. As cars from either direction pass the sign, their

1.

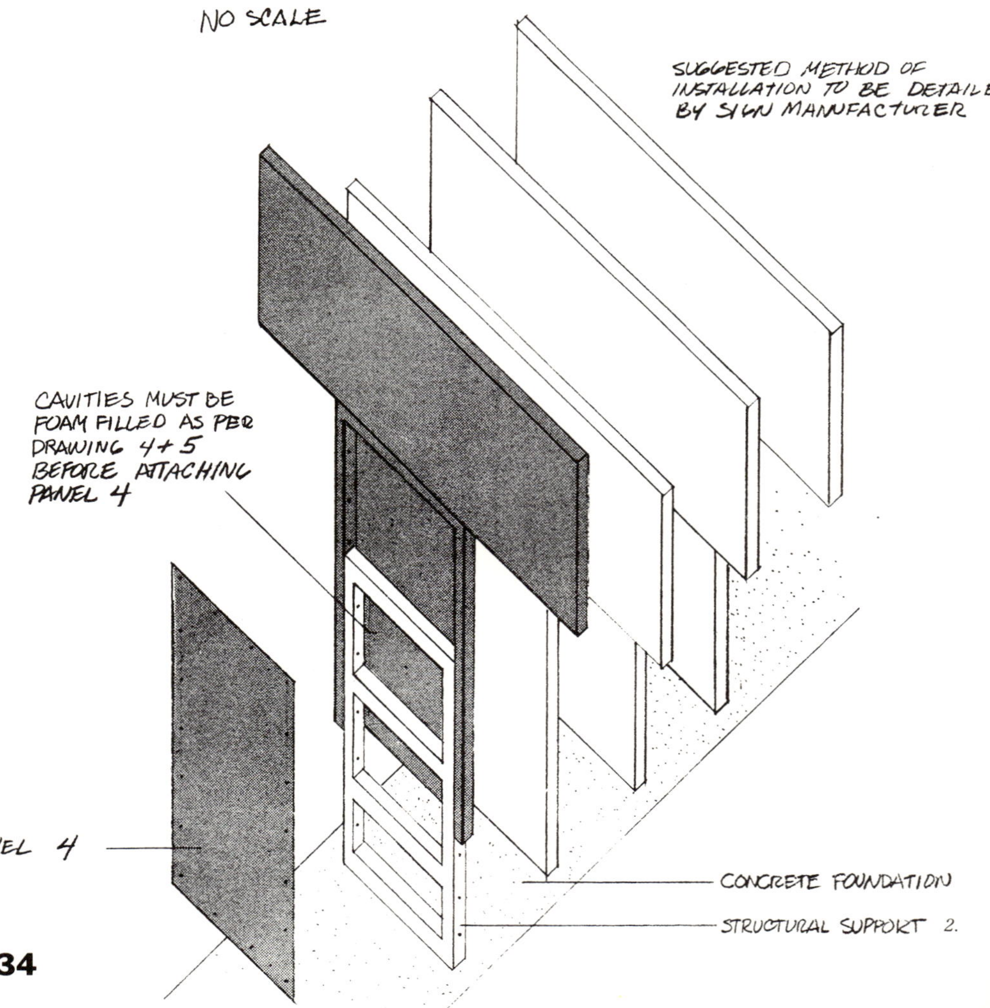

2.

drivers' and passengers' perception of the sculpture is of a pattern of 2″ blades—a totally different visual experience than the longer view.

Initially, more conventional solutions, such as flags or some form of entrance pylon, were investigated, but were rejected because they did not provide the visual mass and drama of the sculptural T's. Constructed of aluminum with concrete footings, the 8′-high by 6′ (maximum width) by 2″-deep T's are as strong and durable as they look. Lettering is Times Roman Bold and Helvetica. The color palette of green to blue was selected to soften the effect of the sign against the surrounding landscape without minimizing its drama or compromising its impact on the potential tenant. The project has been quite well covered in the real estate press and has led to other related commissions for the designers.

. Eight-foot-high aluminum T's in a parallelogram configuration and painted in gradations of green to blue form a dramatic, sculptural entrance sign and advertisement for this office park.

Client: Robert Martin Co. (Elmsford, NY)
Design firm: Gottschalk + Ash International, New York City
Designer: Kenneth Carbone, principal and project designer
Fabricator: White Plains Sign Corp.

3.

Philip Morris
Operations Center

Since the owners and architects of this building knew from the beginning that an art program would be an integral element of the design, Chermayeff & Geismar were hired at an early stage to develop the art along with the evolution of the architecture. The building, in Richmond, Virginia, houses 1300 people and a variety of functions, including administrative and engineering offices, research and quality-control labs, as well as a pilot plant for manufacture of sample products. It is clad in clear anodized aluminum trim and bright red entry porticoes.

Aluminum was, logically enough, a dominant material in the art program. Three 40′-high, bright-red aluminum sculptures—formed, respectively, from cubes, cylinders and tetrahedrons—are set in the pond to establish a dramatic counterpoint to the buildings and provide a focus for the outdoor spaces.

Inside, five 28′-by-28′ aluminum screens in a variety of colors are hung along a central atrium, where they serve to mark the main entrance and each of four circular stairways. Their colors—white, navy blue, teal, burgundy and terra cotta—establish the color of the particular building zone, which is repeated in the stairwell walls and some of the systems office furniture. The screens are made of alucabond shapes joined with nautical swivels.

Chermayeff & Geismar also created two murals for the cafeteria which consist of plywood geometric forms with colored neon tubes mounted behind the shapes. One is 9′ by

1.

1. Skylit alucobond screens in the atrium reinforce the color-coding and mark the main entrance to the complex as well as four stairways to the second level.
2. Three bright-red aluminum sculptures are placed in the pond to provide a dramatic counterpoint to the natural aluminum architecture.

18'; the other 20' by 28'. Twelve 9'-by-28' canvases in gradations of the basic color palette are hung in strategic locations to complete the art program and emphasize the use of color as an enlivenment and aid to orientation. The jury felt that the sympathetic integration of art and architecture successfully demonstrated that a hi-tech work environment can be both vibrant and comfortable to be in.

3, 4. Two cafeteria murals consist of plywood forms and neon tubes.

3.

4.

Client: Philip Morris, Inc. (New York City)
Design firm: Chermayeff & Geismar Associates, New York City
Designers: Ivan Chermayeff, principal; Keith Helmetag, associate
Architect: Davis, Brody & Associates
Fabricators: Lippincott, Inc. (aluminum sculptures); Design and Production (neon murals); Rathe Productions (airbrushed walls); Treitel Gratz (alucabond screens)

RKO Kingsway Theater Mural

The opening of a fourth cinema at the Kingsway Quad Theater in Brooklyn provided the opportunity for a celebratory wall painting. It was RKO's chairman, Mike Landes, who suggested the idea of a mural, and the design firm of Evergreene Painting Studios who decided to make this not so much a celebration of the movie industry, but of Brooklyn itself. By using elements that were typical of Brooklyn and its vital mixture of ethnic neighborhoods, and combining all these in a beautifully executed trompe l'oeil mural, Evergreene has been able to create the kind of living street art that heightens residents' awareness of the cultural richness of their environment.

Says designer Jeffrey Greene, "We traveled up and down Coney Island Avenue, Brighton Beach, Flatbush Avenue, and so on, searching for store fronts and figures to photograph which we felt captured that slightly romantic, older view of Brooklyn. After many rolls of film, we synthesized store fronts and slice-of-life scenes from our subjective memories with the photos. These served as the main focus of the large east wall at street level. Silhouettes of figures waiting for the "El" (elevated railroad) run along the length of the enclosed theater fire escapes, and residential buildings—showing the infinite variety of brick patterns typical of Brooklyn residential architecture—run along the top of the wall.

As a lighthearted touch, Evergreene included signatures and portraits of themselves in

1.

2.

3.

1. Trompe-l'oeil mural makes a feature of the old fire-escape.

2, 3. Simulated storefronts are so real and so authentically ethnic that passersby have been known to stop and try to buy from them.

Athen's
FISH MARKET

DR MURPHY
NUTRITIONIST
SHOE SERVICE
O'Sullivan
INVISIBLE   SOULING
SHOE SERVICE
O'Sullivan
REPAIR
LAZAREV'S
MAGIC SHOE SHO

CHEON   ICE CREAM   ICE CREAM   STATIONERY
Maer's   Maer's
FOUNTIAN   CANDY   SODAS   Maer's
ICE CREAM

VEGETABLES   EVERGREENE GARDEN   FR

4.

5.

6.

7.

the storefronts. For example, their entire staff can be seen eating a giant pie in Martinelli's pizza palace. They also received much advice from an articulate street audience, some of which they incorporated. For example, Jack Lipsky, a student at a local Yeshiva, gave them the name "Eppes Zis" (a little something sweet) for the Jewish bakery, and the Hebrew motto "t'g' zhen" (to your health) for the window. In this way, the local residents brought the mural to life, even to the extent of sometimes stopping and trying to buy something at one of the trompe l'oeil stores, in an unconscious tribute to the realism of the art.

The witty style of the mural deliberately recalls the highly decorated movie palaces of the 1920s and 1930s. And, since the Kingsway was once the home of live vaudeville, its front has been painted to resemble the old Ziegfeld Theater, which until 1964 stood at 54th Street and 6th Avenue in Manhattan. In this, too, neighborhood comments were influential. The modesty of the orthodox Jewish mothers, vociferously expressed, obliged the bare-breasted female statue next to the tragic mask to appear in more decorous attire in the final painted version!

8.

9.

4-8. Community participation helped the designers make the mural into genuine neighborhood street art. As a witty touch, the designers included caricatures of themselves in the storefronts. The whole crew is depicted in the pizza parlor (Fig. 8).

9. Painted ticket booth enhances ticket window.

10. Graphic treatment is intended to express the vitality of the Brooklyn neighborhood and evoke the vaudeville era.

Client: RKO Century Warner (New York City)
Design firm/fabricator: Evergreene Painting Studios, Inc., New York City
Designers: Jeff Greene, Stephen Lazarev

10.

The Aga Khan Hospital and Medical College

American architects and designers working in other lands are learning how to learn from the cultures they embrace. Instead of imposing western attitudes, techniques and styles in a cavalier fashion on countries of the Third World, they are beginning to incorporate local traditions of craftsmanship, materials and art forms into their work—in many cases with very sympathetic results. Throughout Islam, strong impetus in this direction has been given by the Aga Khan, who, in his award programs and in the building projects he directly sponsors, is continually searching for architectural forms and design themes that combine the benefits of modern technology with indigenous values that have endured through the ages.

The 700-bed Aga Khan Hospital and Medical College in Karachi, designed by Boston architects Payette Associates, is an enlightened example of this approach. Its vocabulary of courtyards, screens, wind scoops, terra cotta roofs and integrated ornament is in the finest traditions of Islam. And these themes have guided the sensitive development of the graphic identity and sign system designed by Herman and Lees Associates, who worked extremely closely with both architects and client.

Based on field trips to Pakistan and an extensive review of local crafts, materials and production methods, a palette of teak, marble, brass and porcelainized steel was selected. Furthermore, local textiles were used for banners and local ceramic tile as ornamental accents, which at

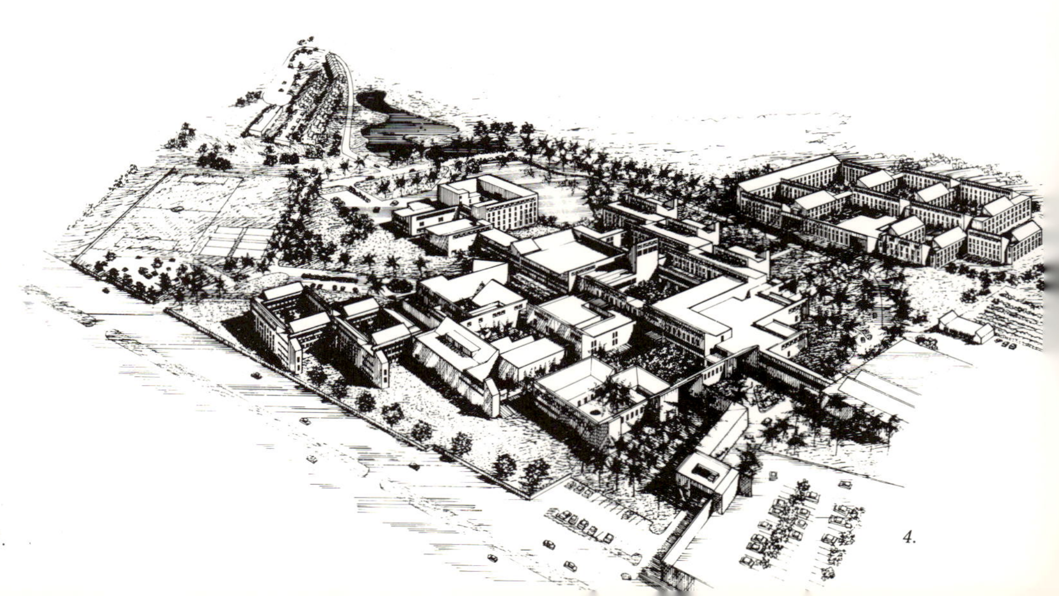

the same time contribute to a functional color-coding system. Although English is the "working" language in the hospital, all signs are also rendered in Urdu, the national language of Pakistan.

The fundamental graphic symbol or logotype for the hospital is a red three-crescent design based on the Moslem equivalent of the Red Cross. It is recognized, even by the illiterate, as a symbol of high-level medical care throughout the developing nations. The illiteracy of large numbers of those using the hospital was a factor in the graphic solution and led to a system of color-coding by means of which people can be given colored tags and told to follow similarly colored signs to their destination. Pictographs, which themselves demand a certain level of sophistication, were used only sparingly.

Exterior signing consists of free-standing porcelain-steel sign panels mounted on concrete monoliths, which match the detailing of the walls; and identification signing sandblasted through the textured outer surface of the walls to a smooth surface underneath, in just the same way as the windows are handled architecturally. There are also some banners. Interior signing includes a directory and directional signing using brass letters on teak panels. Identifying signs are accomplished via a range of techniques from direct silkscreening and sandblasting to the application of brass letters and brass card holders on teak doors, and the insertion of colored bands of melamine

5.

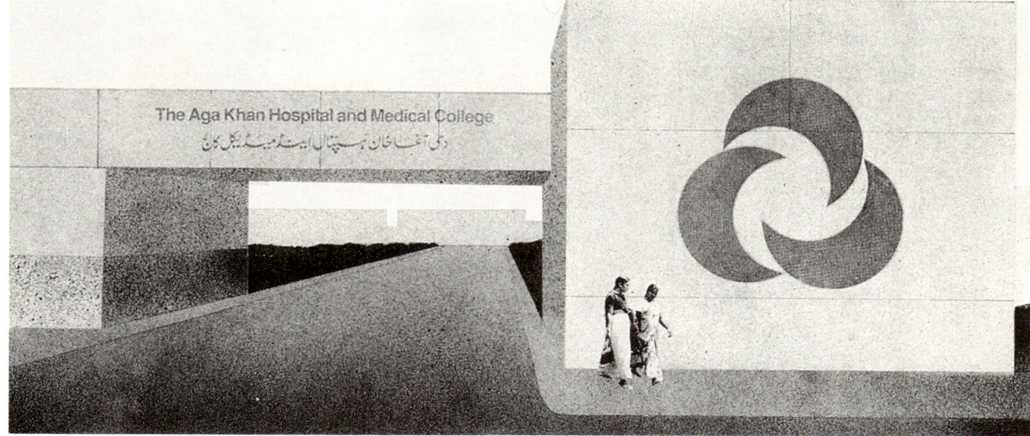

6.

1, 2, 5, 6. The Casebook jury applauded the sensitive use of English and Urdu in all major signs, and the evolution of a symbol, based on the Moslem equivalent of the Red Cross, that can be easily understood by the illiterate.

3, 4. Courtyards and integrated ornament are in the best traditions of Islam.

within the teak. The graphic
system extends to stationery,
official forms, and a series of
very well-handled brochures.

In addition to the Helvetica
and Urdu signs, traditional
calligraphy appears throughout
as an integrated ornamental and
religious element. On a steel
gate, for example, are two
sayings in interlaced Kufic
script. Along the top of the
door is the message, "God is
great, there is no god but God,"
and at the bottom, "Enter
therein in peace and peace will
be upon you." It was this
decorative use of calligraphy
that particulary won the
Casebook jury's admiration.

*7, 8. Kufic calligraphy is integrated with
entrances.*
*9, 10, 12. Exterior signs in English and
Urdu are either porcelain-steel panels on
concrete monoliths or sandblasted directly
into the walls.*
11. Emblem of Aga Khan University.

7.

8.

9.

10.

11.

12.

Client: Aga Khan Hospital and Medical College (Karachi, Pakistan)
Design firm: Herman and Lees Associates, Cambridge, MA
Designers: John Lees, principal; Jon Roll, project designer; Greg Wright, Sarah Speare, Pat Whempner, staff designers; Aale Oayoom, graphics coordinator
Architect: Payette Associates
Fabricators: Letterama, Inc.; Ken Starr (sandblasting)

Rockefeller Center Concourse

When the management of New York's celebrated Rockefeller Center decided they needed a completely new approach to its concourse signing, they wanted it at once. Designers Donovan and Green had only 30 days to develop an acceptable concept, and 60 days to complete the assignment. While it was important for the new signing to be clear and legible "without looking like airport graphics," most essential of all was the need to design a system that would complement the distinguished Art Deco architecture. The designers therefore prepared a checklist of all the existing sign types, made a careful study of the movement of people through the concourse, and then explored new typographical approaches and sign forms. Once they had developed their concept, they produced prototype type selections and gave their clients a six-projector slide show juxtaposing the proposed new signing over the existing concourse. This procedure had the dual advantage of demonstrating the effectiveness of the design and giving the Rockefeller design and management people an excellent presentation tool with which to gain the support of tenants.

Unquestionably, the most important factor determining the design was the character of the architecture—which, say the designers, seemed to demand a palette of black glass, bronze plexiglass, brass and bronze. A black glass fascia was installed above shop windows to tie in with their existing black granite lower facades. All Rockefeller Center building and public signs are bronze and brass, while brass-trimmed dark glass signs identify the various shops and concessions. The whole system has a low-key elegance about it that makes the new signs appear as an integral part of the buildings. A variety of typefaces (including Times Roman and Optima) were used, but Helvetica was maintained on all the main building signs in conformance with the accepted above-ground standard for the Center. Sign boxes are wall-mounted or ceiling-hung, while directories are set in flat to the walls. A hierarchy of sizes begins with small rest-room and elevator/floor signs and moves up to 6' by 12' wall directories. Lettering is consistently green or white for public and Rockefeller Center building signs, but comes in a varied palette for the stores, restaurants and concessions. The rounded corners of the sign hardware are a subtle gesture to the Art Deco theme of the architecture.

The construction schedule was both a challenge and a factor in the successful outcome. It created momentum and forced decisions, especially important in this situation because several design firms had previously attempted to create a new signing scheme without ever reaching an acceptable resolution.

Although no formal post-design evaluation has been undertaken, the designers have found it gratifying to watch people using the concourse and understanding the signs, without recognizing them as new, treating them as an integral part of the architecture.

1.

2.

Client: Rockefeller Center, Inc. (New York City); James Smith, director of design/planning/engineering; Gale Bartlett, display/graphics administrator
Design firm: Donovan & Green, Inc., New York City
Designers: Michael Donovan, Louis Scrima, Eileen Boyer
Fabricator: The Other Sign Co.

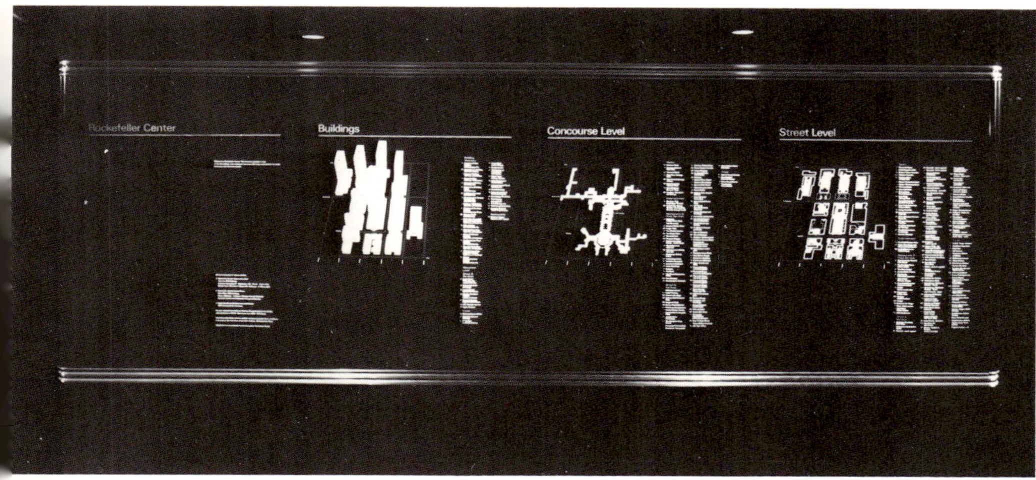

1. *Black glass fascia and sign boxes distinguish tenant from building signs and tie in with existing black granite lower shop facades.*
2. *Brass sign boxes with rounded corners and green or white lettering are used consistently for Rockefeller Center and public signs.*
3. *Directories are set in flush with the walls.*
4. *Art Deco theme of the architecture influenced the sign hardware design, which seems to have become an integral part of the buildings.*

3.

4.

Le Centre Sheraton

Retained only nine months before the opening of this grand, 650-room hotel in Montreal, designers at GSM Design had to prepare themselves to undertake a comprehensive three-part graphics and signing program in very short order. They were responsible for exterior and parking signs; directional and identifying signs within the hotel, which included public areas spread over six floors, and linked by escalators; and printed material, such as menus and wine lists, for all the component bars and restaurants.

Since time for research was so short, and the building was all but completed before they came aboard, the designers conducted much of their preliminary work on-site, making full-scale cardboard and felt-pen models of some of the sign panels, and testing them in place. As a result of these exercises, it became clear to them that, as far as possible, they should use existing architectural surfaces to support the directional signing, rather than erect additional hardware that might compete with the architecture and clutter, rather than enhance, the space.

The principal components of the scheme, then, are brass cut letters applied directly to walls, columns, the escalator enclosure and other architectural surfaces. Supplementing these are brass-covered acrylic or painted metal panels with raised brass lettering giving richness and texture to complement the refined detailing of the interior architecture. A somewhat wider

1.

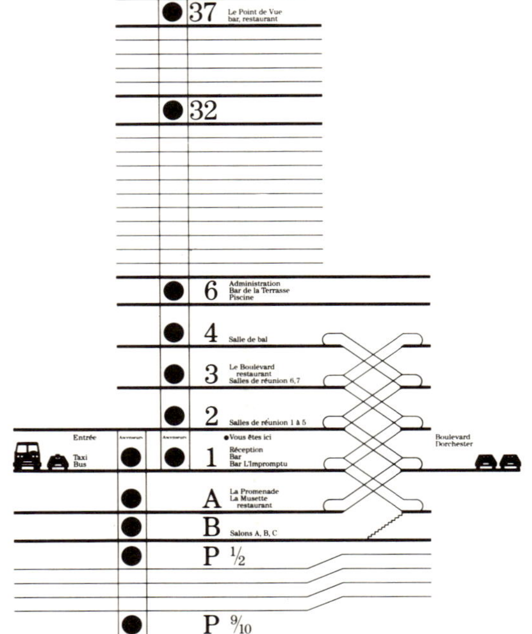

2.

1-3. The structure and vertical analysis of the building are echoed in the directory, which shows the disposal of public areas throughout the hotel.

4-7. Cut brass letters applied directly to walls, and painted-metal or brass-covered acrylic panels with raised letters or pictograms, complement architectural surfaces rather than competing with them for attention.

3.

4.

5.

6.

7.

palette of colors and materials is used to introduce the restaurants and bars; and the printed material is carefully conceived to be compatible with each.

Outside, dark bronze building signs seem at one with the architecture. Green is used to direct traffic to the garage. Once inside, red and blue signs identify each half-level of parking; but all pedestrian signs within the parking areas have a uniform beige background.

In spite of the time crunch, the designers refused to compromise the quality of the scheme they felt most appropriate to the architecture. This meant that there were no short cuts to installation. The brass letters had to be individually cut and applied on all 36 floors of the hotel, but the results, the Casebook jury felt, were well worth the effort.

Century Schoolbook type is used in all public areas inside the hotel, Frutiger for parking and outside directional signing. Individual logos were developed for the restaurants and bars. A materials palette of polished and satin-finish brass, acrylic, enamel, silkscreen, polished stainless steel and wood created just the effect of refined luxury appropriate to a high-class hotel in one of North America's most vital and attractive cities.

8, 11, 12. Restaurant signs are more eclectic, but still elegantly low key.

9, 13. Dark-bronze exterior signs also complement the architecture. Green is used to direct traffic to and from the garage.

10, 14. Hand-cut brass letters are applied with equal effect to different kinds of interior architectural surfaces.

8.

9.

10.

11.

12.

14.

Client: Les Associés Shermas (Montreal); George S. Villedary
Design firm: GSM Design, Inc., Montreal
Architect: Sunkey/Arcop
Fabricator: Simpson's Contract Division

13.

The Connection, Houston

Houston, that city of private verve and public abnegation, has all the virtues and disadvantages of unregulated free enterprise. Its phenomenal growth, unchecked by zoning, has led to excitement, innovation, garishness, confusion and difficulties for the pedestrian in an auto-dominated society. Some of these difficulties have been mitigated by a private tunnel (and skywalk) system, known as "The Connection," composed of a network of predominantly underground passages linking Houston's downtown buildings. Each building owner decides whether or not he wants to connect into the system, and in typical Houston fashion, no architectural standards are imposed to pull the whole thing together. Thus, ceiling heights, corridor widths and colors and finishes vary greatly. Some tunnels include broad lobbies and attractive retail malls; others are blank and unadorned. Furthermore, lack of any coordinated signing has led to great confusion. People were constantly getting lost or winding up facing a blank wall in a dead-end tunnel.

An Ad Hoc Tunnel Committee, formed to try to bring some organization to

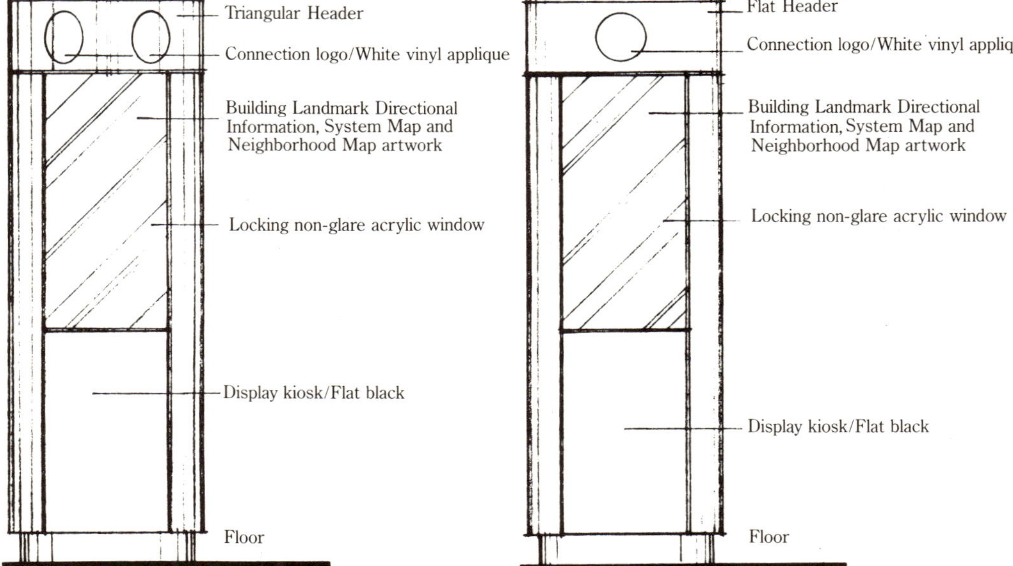

2.

3.

1. *Logo/symbol.*
2, 3. *Drawings of free-standing and wall-mounted kiosks with, respectively, triangular and flat headers.*
4. *A passerby studying one of the wall-mounted kiosks.*
5. *The elements of the kiosk: identity of immediate location and nearby building; system map with neighborhood map identified on it; neighborhood map.*

1.

4.

"The Connection," hired architects and designers 3D/International to create a mapping system that would make the tunnels easier to use. The principal elements of 3D/I's solution are information kiosks, each containing building identification, a system map and a neighborhood map, and a unifying Connection symbol or logo. The kiosks—black to cooperate with the variety of architectural finishes—come in two basic models, free-standing or wall-mounted, but are individually engineered to fit their specific location in the system. They are internally illuminated to stand out in widely varying lighting conditions. Sited at strategic intersections, the 23 kiosks together provide enough information to guide a pedestrian through the entire 3.5-mile tunnel network, if he should choose to go from kiosk to kiosk.

Each kiosk contains: a header identifying the building you have reached and directional arrows to adjacent buildings; a map of the entire system with all tunnels and skywalks coded by map coordinates and cross-referenced alphabetically; and a map of the immediate six-block neighborhood, giving details of access stairs, elevators and escalators, lobbies and major turns and jogs in the system. (The specific kiosk is located on the neighborhood map with a red "you are here" dot. The whole neighborhood map is in turn represented on the system map by a defining red rectangle and kiosk "you are here" dot.)

Kiosk bodies are painted aluminum; maps are duratran

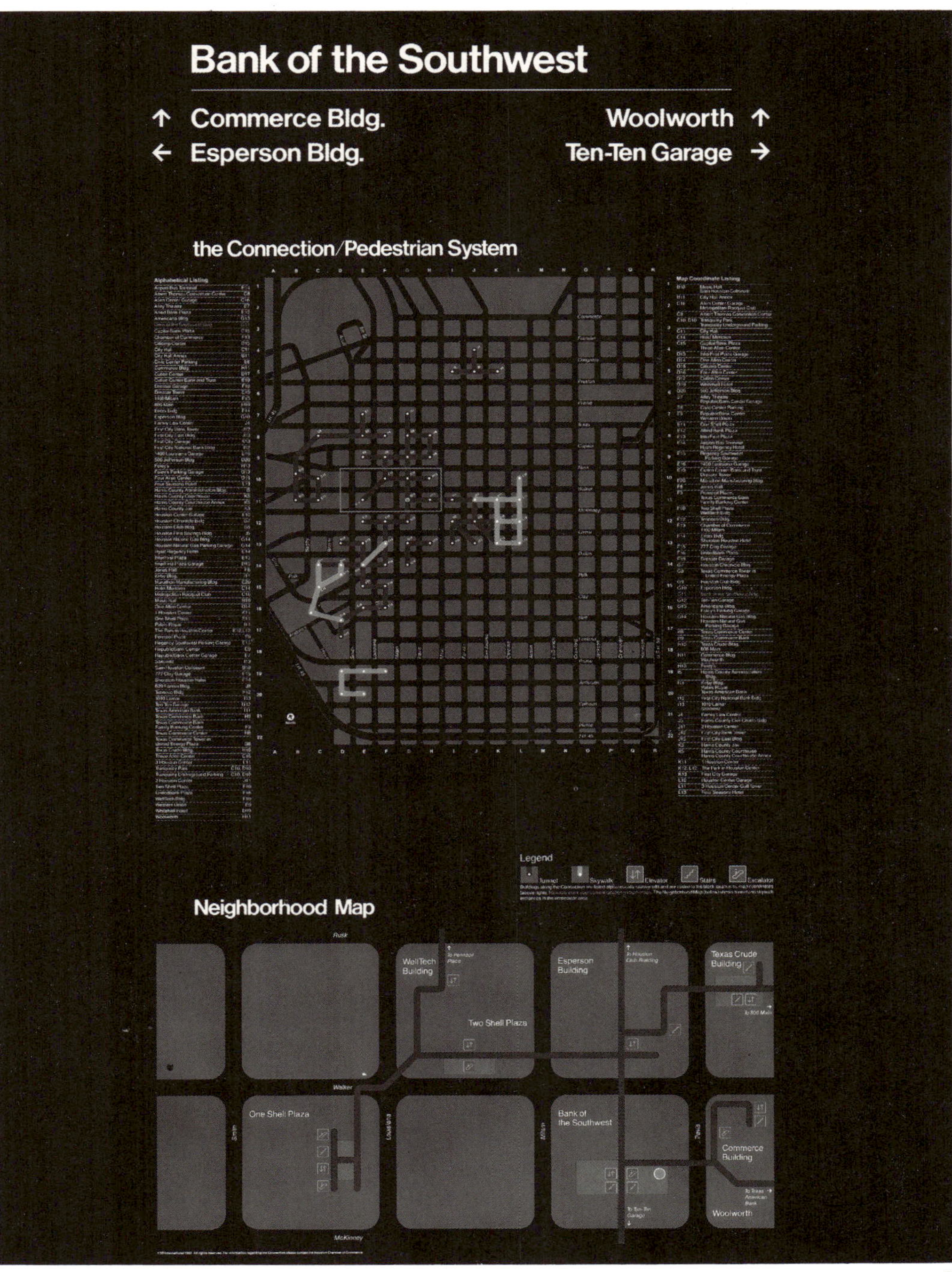

color transparencies—selected for color brilliancy and the ease with which they can be changed. The artwork is mounted behind a locking non-glare acrylic window. Type is Helvetica Regular and Medium; colors are black background, gray for the blocks, dark blue for the tunnels, light blue for skywalks, red for "you are here" dots; and white for type. The Connection symbol is also white. Wall-mounted kiosks are 36⅞" wide by 5′9½" high; free-standing kiosks are 36⅞" wide, but their heights vary according to the ceiling height of their location. Map and information window openings are 4′1½" high by 25⅛" wide.

CRT electronic type display systems were initially investigated but set aside because of their cost. Very few client alterations were made to the system as it developed, but a post-design study among users did result in a lowering of the maps to a more comfortable viewing height; and the incorporation of the red rectangles or "windows" on the system maps to describe the relative location of the specific neighborhood.

The designers were not asked to include street-level identification or supporting trailblazing signs, but they did suggest to their clients that the system would remain somewhat confusing without them.

The Casebook jury thought this a very good graphic resolution of a great deal of information—a plus for pedestrians in a world of hi-tech buildings and cars.

Client: Houston Ad Hoc Tunnel Committee
Design firm: 3D/International, Houston, TX
Designers: Larry Marshall Roberts, senior project designer; Frank F. Douglas, director of graphics division; Dale Willingham, project director; Connection symbol design: Stephen D. Harding; system map design: Stephen D. Harding, Scott Welty; neighborhood map design: Larry Roberts, Stephen D. Harding, Scott Welty; map production: Scott Welty, Mike Parra; production coordinator: Jim Cauthron
Architect: 3D/International
Fabricators: Neon Electric Corp.; San Jacinto Graphics (map fabrication)

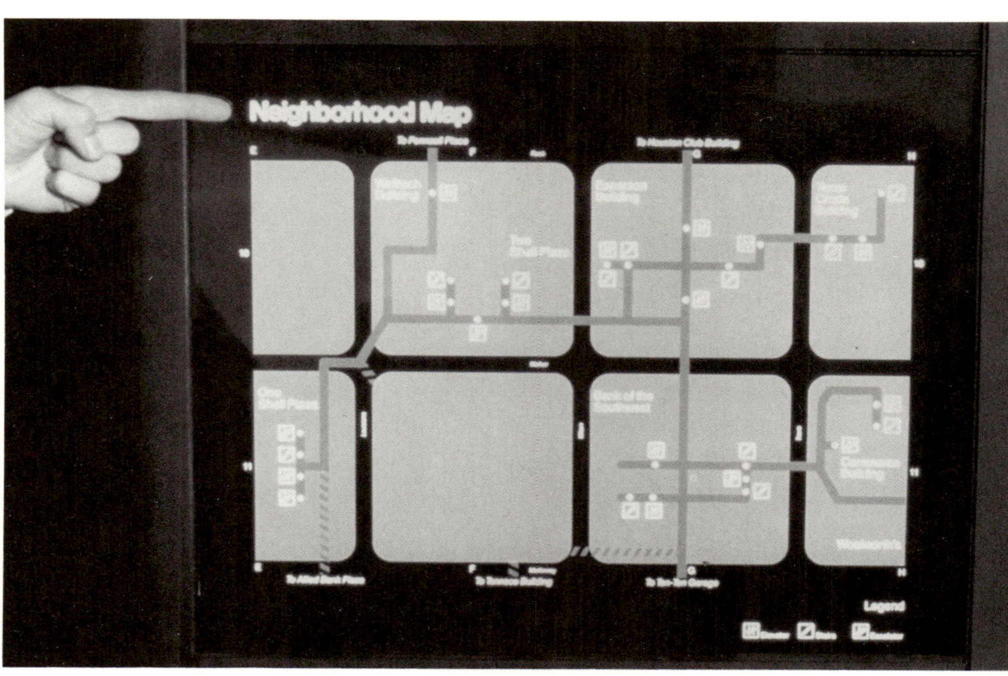

6.

7.

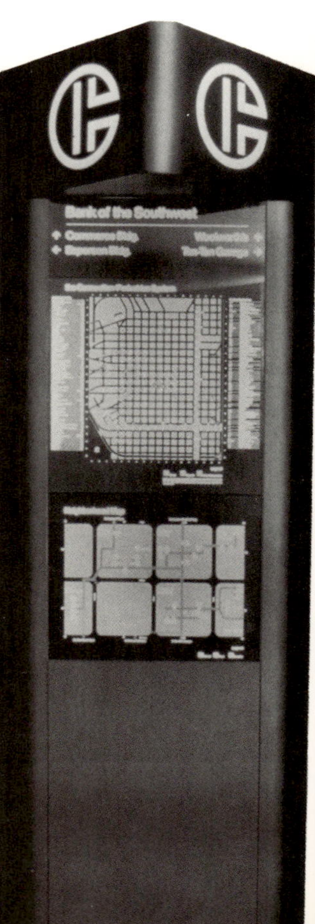

6-8. *Components of the free-standing, triangular header kiosk at the Bank of the Southwest.*

8.

Plane Mate

The very boldness of this solution practically forced the Casebook jurors to vote for it. "Very effective," "deceptively simple," "the right choice," were some of their comments. After all, how could you resist anything so large and red which tells you in no uncertain terms that New York loves you? The first of a fleet of ten 10-year-old people-movers to be rehabilitated by the Port Authority of New York and New Jersey, this clumsy-looking 49′-long vehicle transports up to 150 passengers at a time from planes parked on the apron to the International Arrivals Building at New York's Kennedy Airport.

The sheer size of the vehicle and the need for legibility at great distances dictated the size of the message and the simple clarity of the graphics. In addition to the message "New York Loves You," the vehicle also had to carry an identifying number and the Port Authority logo. Capital letters in the main message are 30″ high; the identifying letter 18″; and the Port Authority logo 5″.

Despite the size of the plane mate, the area available for the message was limited and complicated by the vehicle's design, by the window positions, and by the many bolts, rivets and dents which could not be removed from its side. The white vinyl letters and hearts, which were individually applied by hand, had to be stretched over the bolts and rivets in such a way as to maintain the exact spacing without distorting the characters.

Several different ways of displaying the message were considered, including shortening New York to NY and using the word "loves" instead of the three hearts. A number of type styles, sizes and positions were also reviewed. The final scheme won out because, says designer Diane Whitebay, "it was the most direct, legible and striking solution." White vinyl was specified for the letters and hearts because of its durability and ease of application to large surfaces. Scarlet paint covers the body of the vehicle. Others in the fleet will be painted in equally bold tones of yellow, blue, green, and so on. Clarity and legibility determined the selection of Helvetica Bold as the typeface.

As there were no drawings available, Diane Whitebay had to have measurements taken in the field from the vehicle itself. She also had photographs made of the vehicle with its original color scheme, and a perspective rendering showing the proposed new design, color and type size in exact proportions. A fabrication drawing and a precise mechanical were also produced, the latter to be enlarged and used as artwork.

When the first vehicle was completed and shown to representatives of the airlines whose passengers would be riding in it, no changes at all were suggested for the exterior, although some interior modifications were discussed.

For those arriving at JFK, uncertain of their welcome in the tough city of New York, the sight of this gaily painted blunderbuss proclaiming New York's love should warm the heart and set fears at rest.

1. Up to 150 passengers ride in the plane mate from planes parked on the apron to the International Arrivals Building at Kennedy International Airport.
2. Capital letters in the main message are 30' high.

T
THE PORT AUTHORITY OF NY & NJ
New York

3. Painted brilliant red with white lettering, this is the first of a fleet of ten vehicles to be rehabilitated. Others will be painted in equally bold shades of green, yellow, etc.

Client: Port Authority of New York and New Jersey, Aviation Dept.; Robert J. Aaronson, director
Design firm: Port Authority of New York and New Jersey (New York City), Engineering Dept.; Rino M. Monti, chief engineer
Designer: Diane Whitebay, graphic designer, Design Division
Architect: Sheldon D. Wander
Interior designer: Maria Aasland
Fabricator: Hudson General Aviation Services
Consultant: Port Authority of New York and New Jersey, NY and Central Automotive Division, (General Services Dept.)

3.

T
AEROLINEAS ARG
AEROLINEAS ARGENTINAS
♥ ♥ You

Cincinnati Zoo

The old-fashioned zoo of the tiny wire-mesh, iron-barred and concrete cage is fortunately becoming a thing of the past. Many zoo animals are now allowed to roam in simulations of their natural habitats, and people have to walk a little further to see them. As a corollary of this, graphic design is playing a strong role in directing visitors through the different regions and identifying and describing the species they will find there.

The Cincinnati Zoo—third largest in the U.S.—commissioned designers Schenker, Probst & Barensfeld (after a competitive selection process) to develop a comprehensive design standard for signing, exhibits and printed matter, which must have an essentially homogeneous, naturalistic flavor, but be flexible enough to handle the constantly changing zoo environment and population.

It was a substantial assignment, with a design budget of $55,000, and five discrete phases in the work. The first two, research and conceptual design, and design development have been documented in the form of bound reports, which set out details of alternative directions considered and the reasons for adopting the final approach. The third phase, prototype testing, has also been completed, but phases four and five—the provision of a graphic design standards manual, and the application of the signing to actual zoo exhibits—are still in progress. At the time of the Casebook judging, only the signing in a five-acre area containing the Swan Lake and

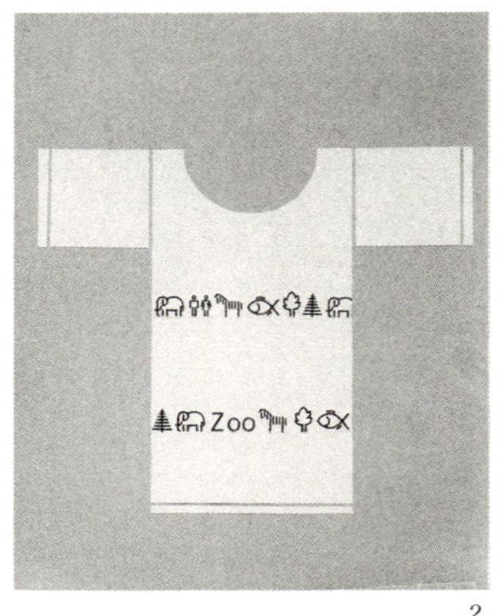

1.

2.

3.

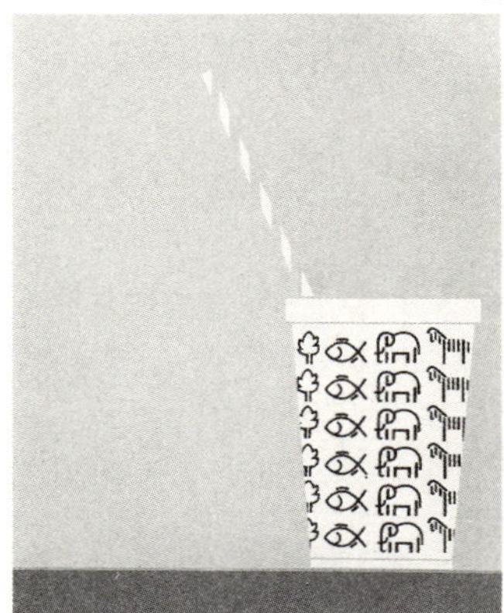

4.

5.

6.

1-6. Frutiger type and witty pictograms appear on numerous signs, documents and artifacts, from T-shirts to paper cups to the zoo newsletter.

7, 8. Panels on poles set right in the water give information about the birds in the Swan Lake section. Metal channels accept changeable modular panels.

9. Animal pictograms.

7.

8.

9.

Exit →
Keep your park clean
← World of Insects
African Veldt ↗
← Carnivore House
← Birds of Prey

Keep your park clean
Strollers →
← Gibbon Island
↙ African Veldt
↙ Baboon-
Aoudad Island
Reptile House ↗

10.

11.

12.

the habitat of the Birds of Prey was fully implemented; it was these signs that attracted the jury.

Two kinds of informational signs are included in each area—modular identifying signs enabling visitors to recognize the birds; and interpretational and educational sign structures that give details of migration, flight patterns, endangered species, and so on. In the Swan Lake, identifying sign structures consist of a series of panels set into a metal channel system fastened to treated-wood poles that can be planted in or near the water. The top (title) unit is a silkscreened illustration plus photo-etched text on aluminum. Below that are fiberglass-embedded cibachrome photographs of the different birds, each with an accompanying photo-etched aluminum text panel. The results are a very pleasing series of sculptural elements that seem quite at home in their natural setting. It is almost as though the pages of a very good bird guidebook have sprung into three-dimensional life. In the Birds of Prey areas, the same kinds of panels are mounted on wood-supported metal channels and set horizontally among the greenery. For both sections, 59½"-high interpretational and educational sign structures are wood-framed or -supported alucobond silkscreened panels containing a wealth of illustrated documentary information.

For directional signs, a color-coding palette (red for caution, yellow for traffic, green for general information, white for exhibitions, black for facilities)

13.

14.

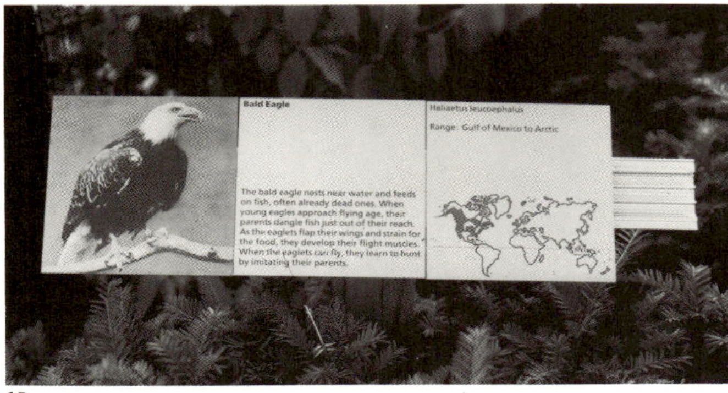

15.

16.

10, 11. *Directional signs are color-coded using a standard post and aluminum panel structural system.*
12. *Zoo information pictograms.*
13-16. *Wood post and horizontal metal channels in the Birds of Prey section enable identifying sign panels to be placed right among the greenery. Panels are photo-etched aluminum.*
17. *Interpretational and educational material is on wood-supported silkscreened alucobond panels.*

17.

is applied against a gray
aluminum background on fairly
standard wood post and
aluminum panel structures.
Throughout the zoo, Frutiger is
the specified typeface, but
many of the signs combine type
and witty pictogram messages.

18.

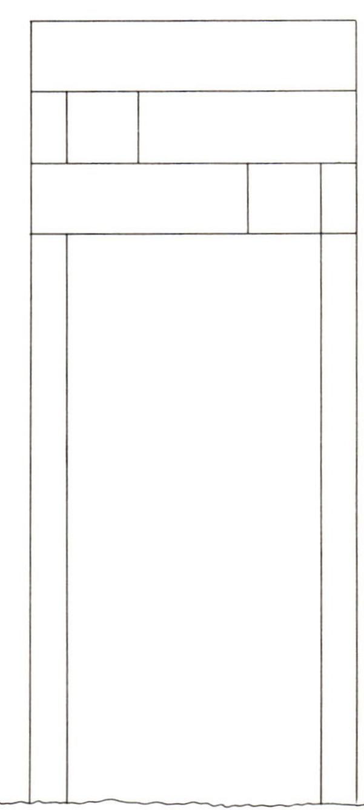

19.

Client: Cincinnati Zoo, Zoological
Society of Cincinnati, OH
Design firm: Schenker, Probst &
Barensfeld, Cincinnati, OH
Designers: Heinz Schenker, Robert
Probst, Mark Barensfeld, Alison Probst,
Mark Minelli
Architects: Glaser & Myers and
Associates, Inc.
Fabricator: Display Sales, Inc.;
Aluminum Extruded Shapes, Inc.; Metal
Photo of Cincinnati, Inc.; Pannier Corp.
(Graphics Div.)

20.

18. Modular plant identification system.
19. Drawings of possible sign configurations.
20, 21. Directional and other signs, based on
carefully worked out typographic grid, are
free-standing or applied to wall surfaces.
Frutiger type is used throughout.

21.

New Rochelle Facade Program

Although the City of New Rochelle, New York, is, to some extent, marooned amid a sea of amorphous shopping malls, its own downtown has a rich repertoire of high and low Victoriana, Art Deco and post-war Modern buildings, which the city recognized had considerable community and commercial potential. But much of the original architecture and decoration was concealed behind false facades, fake stone, and the grime and disrepair of decades of neglect. In 1977, a city-sponsored Facade Improvement Program began to change all that. Starting with a four-building demonstration project, the city is now well along with the renaissance of a 20-block area, and so far more than 100 stores and businesses have received design improvements.

Under the supervision of the City Department of Development, the design firm of Anthony Russell, Inc., was charged with the design and refurbishing of facades, the selection of colors, the graphic design and hardware specification for a multitude of signs—on stores, proclaiming street names, giving parking and pedestrian directional information—in fact, with orchestrating the entire graphic treatment of the streetscape.

The work involved an extensive study of the history of the city and its constituent buildings, as well as interviews with the merchants and businesses concerned. There was also a careful city-approval process. Although no attempt has been made to impose a single architectural or graphic style upon an urban precinct

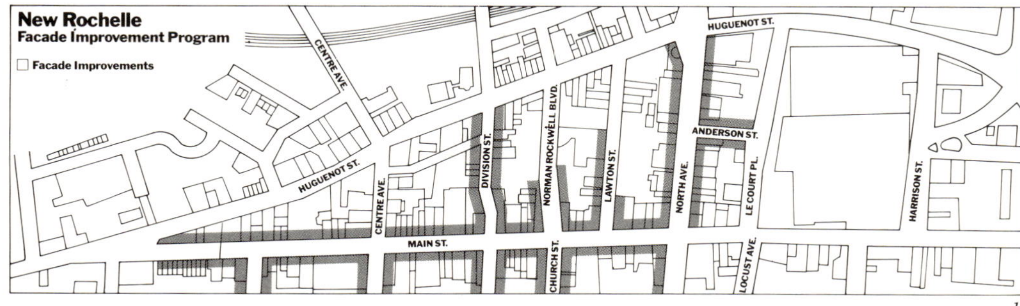

1.

2.

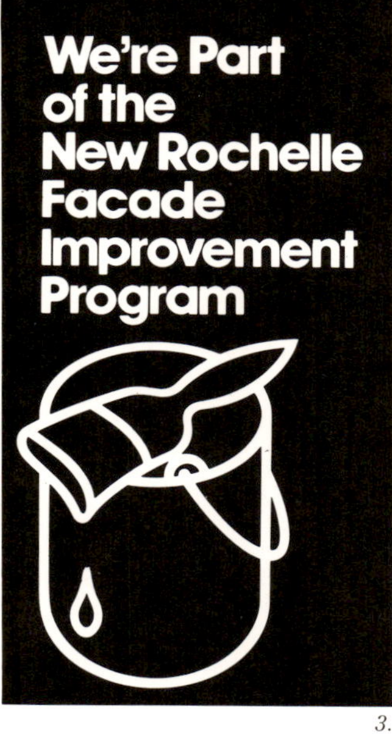

3.

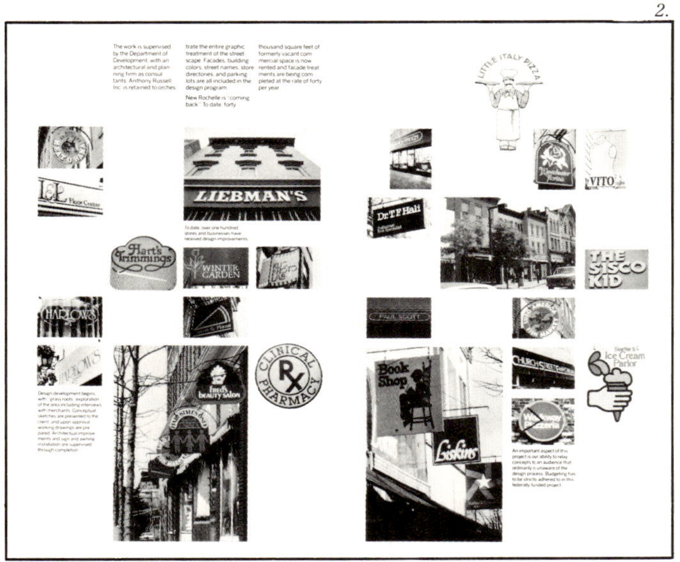

1. Map of improvement area.
2. "Before" view of street scene.
3. Pride in progress.
4. Designer's brochure showing range of New Rochelle signs.

4.

5.

6.

whose richness lies in its diversity, a certain unity or homogeneity has been achieved by means of a compatible color palette, consistency in the scale and positioning of the signs, and the choice of a range of appropriate typefaces.

The program was financed by a Federal Community Development Block Grant—and therefore asks nothing of owners or building tenants except their agreement to maintain the facades as built (or rebuilt) for seven years, unless special city approval be obtained for subsequent alterations.

Since the budget for each store averaged only $1000 to $2000, there is very little use of three-dimensional signs. Strong reliance is placed on paint and sturdy, durable materials such as marine plywood, carved wood, cut plastic and aluminum. To reduce visual clutter on individual store fronts, wherever possible a simple sign with coordinated type and coloring is substituted for the all-too-familiar hodge-podge of graphically unrelated announcements of wares, specialties and departments. Small identifying signs painted directly onto store windows are used throughout the program for quick pedestrian information and as a unifying element. One particularly attractive touch in the renovation of Liebman's store for boys and girls apparel that caught the attention of the jury was the use of a large corner sign (matching the main store sign board) but framed and supported by a heavy Victorian gingerbread bracket.

The jury was most favorably impressed by a very good solution to what the jurors recognized as a difficult assignment. More important than all the information it gives about vendors and their wares, is the overall impression of vitality, renewal and love of the past that such a well-conceived program conveys.

7.

8.

9.

10.

11.

12.

13.

14.

15.

16.

17.

18.

19.

20.

Client: City of New Rochelle (New York), Dept. of Development
Design firm: Anthony Russell, Inc., New York City
Designers: Anthony Russell, Peg Patterson, Casey Clark, Kevin McPhee, Ian McNeil
Architects: Historic Design Associates

Fabricators: Neptune Sign Co.; White Plains Sign Co.; Portchester Shades and Awnings; Acme Awning; Albe Sign Co.
General contractors: Benro Construction Co. (Tom Ceston, president); K. Capolino Design & Renovation Ltd. (K. Capolino, president)

The Market at Citicorp Center

New York's Citicorp Center has been justly praised as a "people place," and indeed it is perhaps the best-used corporate public space in the city. Its dramatic skylit atrium, surrounded by stores and restaurants, was named "The Market" when the building opened, and has become well-known in the city as a place to go for coffee and croissants, fettucini alfredo, or just to sit and read the paper. Its reputation—given a fillip by successful initial publicity and maintained through word-of-mouth by regular patrons—needed recharging a few years down the line. One good way of doing this was to make The Market entrances much more clearly visible in the streetscape, and designers Gottschalk + Ash were hired to do just that.

After an extensive analysis of vehicular and pedestrian traffic around and through the building, a review of the plans, and photo studies of the architecture, a model was constructed to provide a reference for alternative sign configuration proposals. Key program requirements were: visibility from a number of vantage points within a two-block radius; compatibility with the architecture of the building; "retail impact"; and economy of installation.

The final concept, which had to be approved by several levels of management within Citibank, is a series of three-entrance sign structures, each composed of a number of 45-degree triangular panels of bright red-painted, perforated aluminum sheet on a structural frame. The panels are spread 2′ apart and anchored at each corner to three supporting aluminum tubes. The message "The Market at Citicorp Center" in Helvetica Light and Bold Italic is fabricated of ¼″ aluminum, painted white and mounted to the end panels of each sign. Spacing between the panels allows light to penetrate the glass entry facades.

These signs have great impact without being disruptive, and considerable visual mass without comparable weight. This was important because, due to the scale of the signs, weight distribution, wind loading and structural stress on the building had to be carefully studied. The size also somewhat complicated installation, which required drilling and cutting the building facade to receive the sign anchors. The two side-entrance signs are 21′ wide by 10′ high; the third, at the corner entrance on 54th Street and Third Avenue, is 24′ wide and 7′6″ high. The red triangular emblem appears again on a more conventional post and panel sign marking the main entrance to the office tower.

The designers feel that the triangular theme of the signs, which takes up the dramatic angled roof of the building, has helped to integrate them successfully with the architecture—and the Casebook jury concurred. The choice of aluminum was also, of course, an appropriate complement to the gleaming aluminum building skin.

1.

2.

1. *Post and panel sign identifies The Market at the main entrance to the office tower.*
2-4. *Bright red aluminum triangles identify chief entrances to The Market. Triangular form picks up rakish Citicorp roof configuration and red complements natural aluminum building skin.*
5. *Directory in the atrium identifies component eateries and other concessions.*

Client: Citibank (New York City); Elizabeth Sapery
Design firm: Gottschalk + Ash International, New York City
Designers: Kenneth Carbone, principal designer; Steve Orant, senior designer; Julie Koch-Beinke, junior designer; Josh Scharf, technical adviser
Architect: Hugh Stubbins & Associates, Inc.
Fabricator: Studio 13
Consultant: Stanley Goldstein, structural and civil engineering

3.

4.

5.

Macomber Farm

Man's inhumanity to man is only surpassed by his brutality to animals. Not content with hunting, trapping and clubbing them, boiling them alive, or experimenting on them in laboratories, we have conceived of factory farming methods, the more cruel of which deprive them even of movement and the light of day in the interests of the voracity or refinement of the human appetite. Recognizing and deploring many of these realities, Macomber Farm and Education Center in Framingham, Massachusetts, is an effort to educate the human species to deal more kindly with the creatures it exploits. John Macomber (wealthy Boston businessman and animal lover) left his farm to the Massachusetts Society for the Prevention of Cruelty to Animals for just the purpose of sensitizing people to the needs of animals. He believed with MSPCA's founder, George Angell, that "a thousand times more can be done to prevent cruelty by humane education than by any other means."

After a long gestation period (Macomber died in 1955), the MSPCA in 1977 commissioned Boston architects Shepley, Bullfinch, Richardson and Abbott to plan the site and develop a series of barns, each of which is divided into two areas—an open exhibit space and a shelter for the animals displayed there. The highly original exhibit program is the work of Edwin Schlossberg, who in turn hired Keith Godard, partner in the New York design group Works, to devise a comprehensive signing and graphics program which would integrate the diverse program

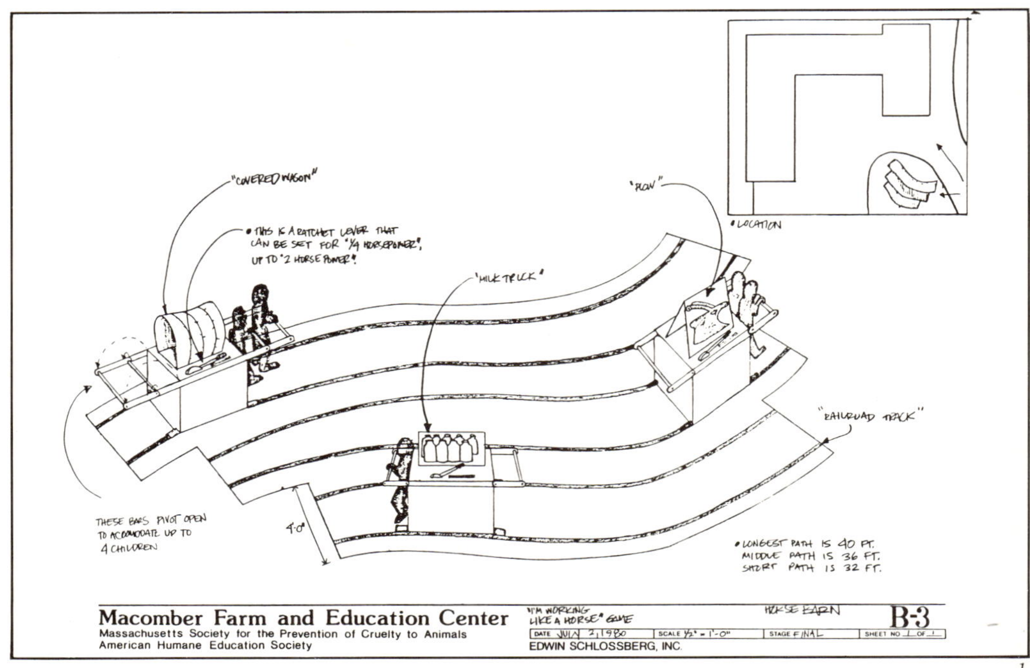

1.

2.

3.

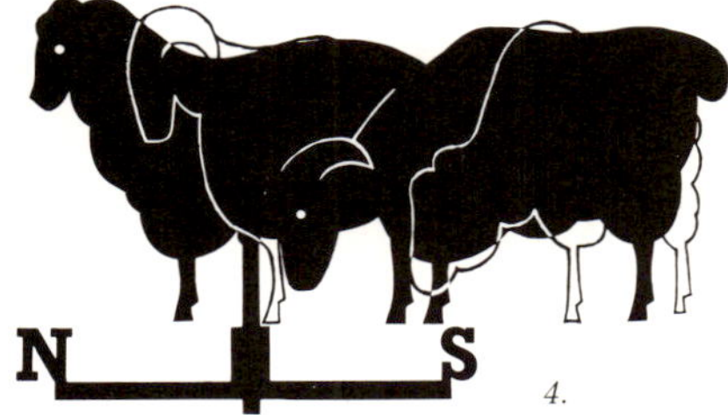

4.

5.

6.

7.

8.

MacomberFarm

9.

1. *Diagram from Edwin Schlossberg's proposal for "I'm Working Like a Horse" game.*
2. *Electronic program announcement.*
3. *Information kiosks have porcelainized enamel top panels detailing daily life cycle of animals in barns. Other panels include considerable information—among them, a glossary, special events panel and map. Braille signs on kiosk are stamped metal with vinyl coating.*
4. *Cattle and sheep barn weathervane.*
5-8, 12-15. *Stylized but realistic shapes symbolize animals and equipment.*
9. *Reception center. Panels depict human hand as an important means of communication with animals.*
10. *Cattle barn entrance sign. Panel backgrounds are in light green and blue.*
11. *Close-up of horse barn information kiosk. Braille signs are uniformly red, identifying them for the partially sighted.*

10.

11.

12.

13.

14.

15.

elements, and inform and entertain the public.

MSPCA's original notion that the exhibits should focus on man's cruelty to animals was abandoned at Schlossberg's urgent suggestion as being too horrible to contemplate. Instead, Schlossberg conceived an elaborate visitors' tour, and invented a series of participatory games and demonstrations which would encourage visitors to identify with the needs and behavior of the animals housed on the farm. Thus, in addition to the signs and panels directing people to the barns and, once they were inside, describing to them facts about the animals, environmental conditions and humane methods of treatment (as well as describing cruel practices which ought to be outlawed, such as imprisoning calves in small crates to be fattened for veal), the graphics program had to embrace information kiosks and numerous indoor and outdoor games—some of them computerized. These invite people to see or work like animals, find their way by scent or sound and communicate in the same ways animals do.

The challenge for Godard and his partners, Stephanie Tevonian and Hans van Dijk, was to bring order to what might easily become a chaos of animal experiences, and to do this within the short seven-month time period allowed them to accomplish all the work.

With simplicity as their catchword, the Godard team devised basic animal identifying shapes and colors for each animal type, which could be used on all signs and panels relating to that species. They selected Rockwell as an easily legible serif typeface, and made heavy use of the Federal Express service to rush mechanicals to the fabricator in Boston. Clear, simple colors were chosen for all descriptive signs—which are either white on blue, black and white, or black and a color. Braille signs are uniformly red, since red is the most readily identifiable color for the partially sighted. Weather- and vandal-resistance influenced the choice of porcelain enamel, stamped metal with vinyl coating, and silkscreening with epoxy enamel ink as the fundamental materials palette. All have worked out well, although Godard would like the chance to paint in gray the bare wood frames of some of the kiosk signs, which got wrongly specified in the rush to meet the deadline.

In the face of the farm's fundamentally grim message that human beings have savagely mistreated animals—and still mistreat them—Godard was anxious that the animals themselves should come through as wholly delightful. The animal pictures that appear on 8' backlit signs, pictographic panels and even zoetropes, although anatomically accurate, have an element of whimsicality about them, which led to some discussion among the Casebook jurors. Their verdict was, however, generally very favorable, particularly because the exhibits are so involving for the visitors.

16.

17.

18.

19.

20.

16. Octagonal goat barn. Panel on fence
identifies barn by depiction of man milking
goat.
17-20, 25-28. Aspects and antics of the horse.
21. Panels on horse barn wall giving facts
about the horse and how to treat him.

22. Entrance sign characterizes the spirit of
Macomber Farm.
23. Computerized questions and answers
provide visitors with supplementary
information.

24. Visitors watch chicken gestures on a screen
and guess what they mean in the pecking
order saga.

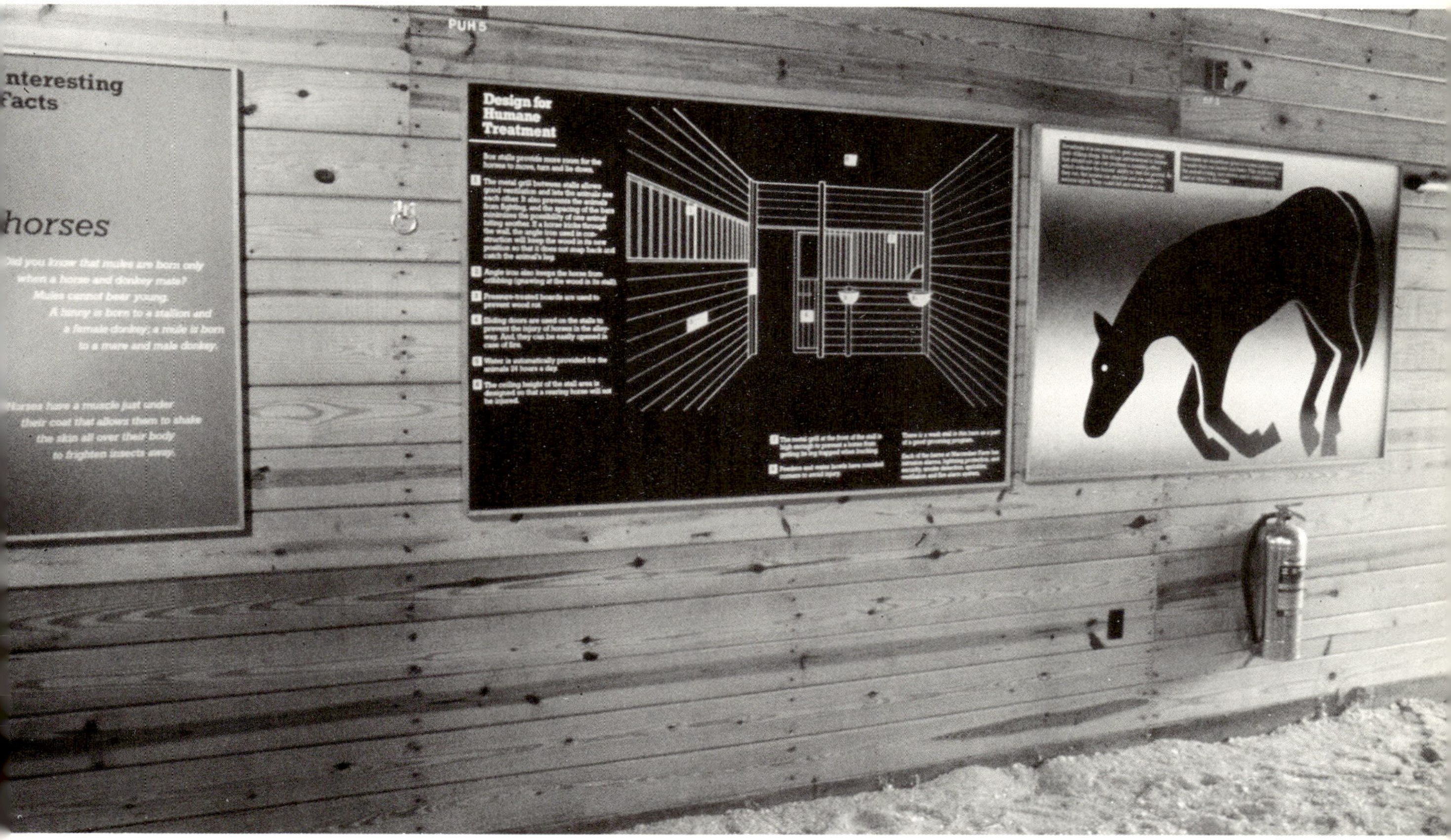

21.

Client: Massachusetts Society for the
Prevention of Cruelty to Animals,
(Boston)
Design firm: Works, New York City
Designers: Keith Godard with
Stephanie Tevonian and Hans van Dijk
Assistant designers: Jeri Froelich,
Linda Procaccino, Julia Bredbenner, Greg
Elkin and Pamela Shaw
Concept and exhibit designer:
Edwin Schlossberg, Inc.
Architect: Shepley, Bullfinch,
Richardson and Abbott
Fabricator: Target Communications

22.

23.

24.

25.

26.

27.

28.

Braker Center

"Bold, simple, handsome" are adjectives graphic designers often use to describe their own work, but the Casebook jury thought they could be justly applied to the environmental graphics for this business park in Austin, Texas. By dividing the complex into four segments, giving each a color which is displayed on building fascia and window mullions, directional signs, and most strikingly on 10′-high identifying pylons, designers Creel Morrell have imparted color, cohesion and a certain distinction to a group of low-key, one-story buildings.

Retained at the time of ground-breaking, the designers had nine months and a design budget of $15,000 to accomplish their task. They conducted numerous site reviews, created preliminary sketches and then—rejecting a system of horizontal building markers—made a model for on-site viewing of the vertical solution. Legibility from moving vehicles and resistance to extreme Texas weather conditions were prime considerations, as was the client's desire to make some kind of positive impact on a flat site. In addition to the seven nylons, there are four 5′-high by 12′-long by 8″-thick main entry signs; one secondary sign two-thirds the size; and 11 8′3″-high directional signs with bold arrows as well as numerals.

Free-standing sign structures are iron-framed with spray-painted, sheet-metal faces and scotchlite numerals, letters and arrows. Helvetica regular is used on all pylons and directional signs—in white, on red, orange, blue or green backgrounds.

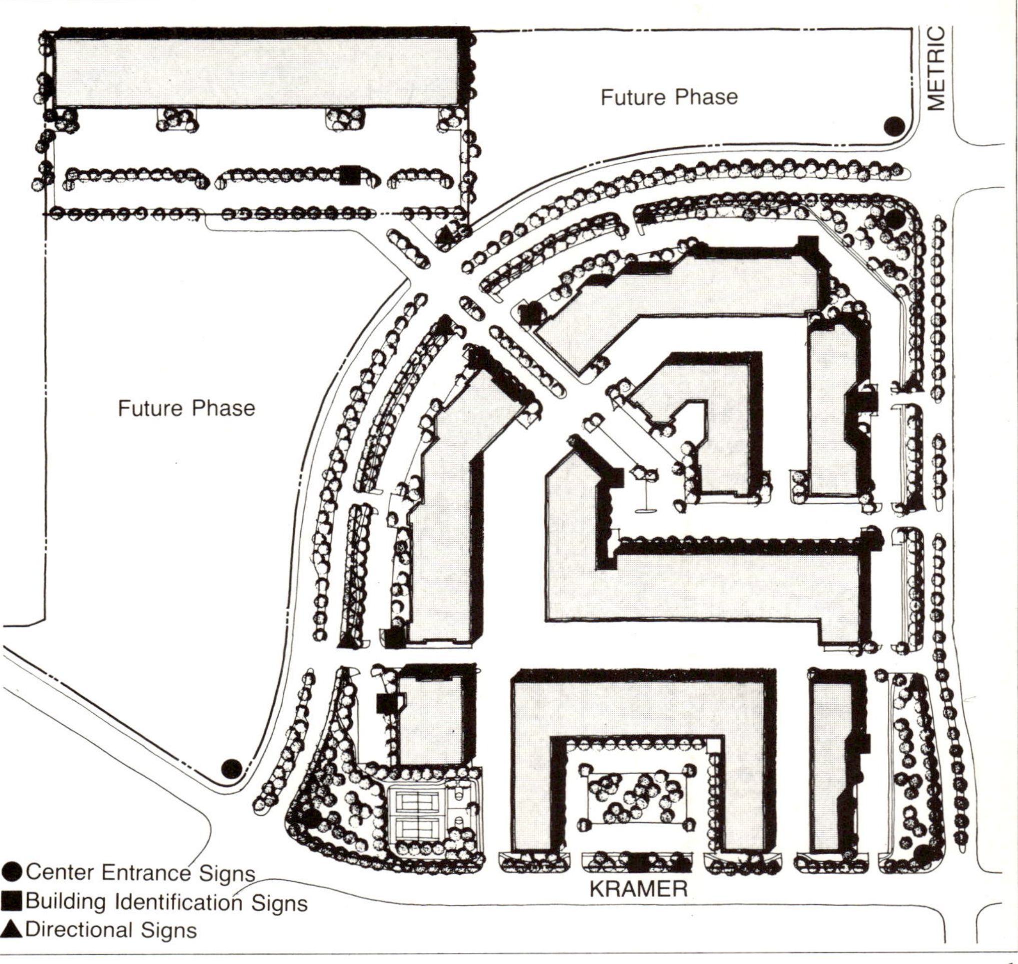

1.

2.

1. Map of business park showing location of the signs.

2. Main entrance monolith.

3, 4. There are 11 8′3″ high directional signs, color-coded with arrows as well as numerals.

5, 6. The 11 identifying pylons are 10′ high. Colors are repeated on building fascia and window mullions.

Client: The Trammell Crow Co. (Austin, TX); Sandy Gottesman, managing partner
Design firm: Creel Morrell, Inc., Houston, TX; Eric G. Morrell, vice president/design
Fabricators: J.F. Zimmerman & Sons, Inc. (building identification signs and directionals); Neon Electric
Consultant: Bill Sawyer & Associates (technical assistance)

12
30
32

24
24

44

30

The streets of Portland, Oregon have been enlivened by a dazzling painted bus, which cruises the city picking up passengers who want to visit any one of three major Tri-Met centers of culture and knowledge relating to the resources of the universe. The Western Forestry Center, the Washington Park Zoo and the Oregon Museum of Science and Industry are equally represented on the body of the bus, whose super-realistic images evoke some of the wonders of the universe. Animals from the zoo, the planet Jupiter, spacecraft, a section through a Douglas fir tree are boldly, if not brashly, painted on the bus against a vivid sky background. The sky changes from midday at the front to night at the back— where a head-on view of a tiger brings to mind the opening lines of Blake's poem:

*Tiger, tiger burning bright
In the shadow of the night
What immortal hand or eye
Could frame thy fearful
symmetry?*

The limited budget—only $5000 for design and $25,000 for painting the bus—did not inhibit the results. The major problem for the designers was posed by the need to deal creatively with wheels, windows and doors and with the

1.

2.

3.

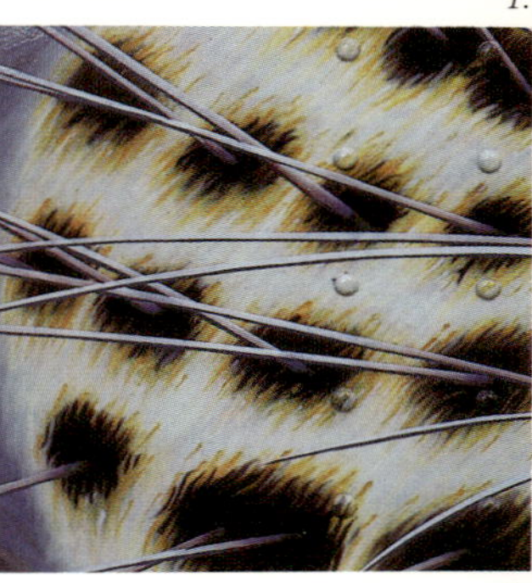

4.

5.

1. Tiger head-on.
2. Section through a tree trunk.
3. Cloud formation.
4. Close up of tiger's whiskers.
5. Animals beneath the planets.
6, 7. Painted layouts for design of sides of bus.

ribbed and riveted surface of the bus, all of which was solved by patience and care in the painting.

Designers Scott and Cheryl McIntyre conceived the design, painted a scale model of the bus and did the fine airbrush detailing and gold-leaf lettering on the bus themselves. They used automotive lacquers for ease of spraying, accented by pearlescent paints and gold and silver leaf, which create an almost psychedelic presence. Thus, an ordinary city bus has become a kinetic sculpture, outrageous perhaps, but hard to resist on its own account, let alone for the lure of its destinations. Public reaction has been good, and museum/zoo/ forestry center business is up.

Client: Tri-Met's Washington Park Zoo; Oregon Museum of Science and Industry; Western Forestry Center (Portland, OR)
Design firm: Scott & Cheryl McIntyre, Portland, OR
Designers: Scott McIntyre, Cheryl McIntyre
Painting: Jack Ruckman, Dale Figley, Scott McIntyre
Fabricator: The Beard Paint Shop

8.

9.

10.

11.

12.

8. Trees and clouds.
9. Objects in space.
10. The crouch of the panther.
11, 12. Painted layout for design of back and front of bus.
13. The bus in action with balloons.

13.

White Marsh Mall

"The Pic-Nic" is a cluster of 22 food-related shops surrounding a central skylit seating area on the second level of the White Marsh Shopping Mall in suburban Baltimore. It needed an attractive entrance sign, as well as individual tenant (and service) signs, which would tie the complex together, while identifying and characterizing the gastronomic emphasis of each of the component shops. RTKL, architects for the entire shopping mall, were also responsible for the graphics, whose design and execution were entrusted to Phil Engelke with Judy Staples.

The main entrance sign, executed in porcelain-enamel, takes the form of an 8' by 4' canopy with marquee lights and "The Pic-Nic" in striking white, red and orange neon lettering. The individual hand-painted 3'-square shop signs—reminiscent of the old trade signs found in Europe—are unified by a common dark-green and white checkerboard motif. Belwe Medium was the selected typeface, chosen for its period character, also evoked by the porcelain enamel, neon and marquee lights.

The jury voted the project in because they enjoyed the lighthearted character of the sign illustrations. These—ranging from a white cock and hen to a large strawberry, to a chef carrying a pie, to a very pink pig—are not remarkable for their subject matter, but

2.

1.

3.   4.   5.   6.

7.

1. Approach to the Mall.
2-6. Green and white checkerboard motif
surrounds and unifies illustrative signs
identifying the various eateries.
7. "Pic-Nic" entrance sign and view looking
down into skylit atrium.

have a stylized freshness that is altogether appealing. The work involved careful discussion and coordination with each of the shop tenants, and the creation of models to ensure that the signs were positioned for maximum visibility from the main mall.

8.

9.

8, 9. Hanging signs have Old World charm.
10, 11. Location and site plans from The Rouse Company's White Marsh Mall brochure.

White Marsh, in the center of
Baltimore's high growth, northeast
corridor, is within easy reach of
the Baltimore Beltway (I-695),
the John F. Kennedy Expressway
(I-95) and other major arterials
serving the region.

Locally, the site is served by
White Marsh Boulevard, Silver
Spring Road, Perry Hall and
Honeygo Boulevards.

The site is an integral part
of a 1,500-acre, comprehensively
planned town center development. In addition to 132 acres
for retail use, White Marsh will
contain concentrations of office,
industrial, commercial, service
and residential uses.

- ■ Commercial
- ▣ Office and Industrial
- ■ Residential

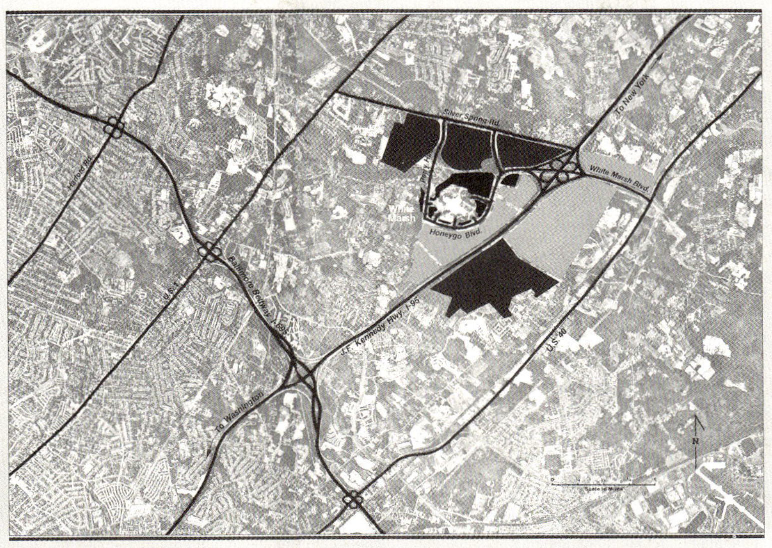

10.

SITE

The five-department store plan,
enclosed in a complete ring road,
provides easy pedestrian access
on four sides and two levels.

- ■ Commercial
- ▣ Office and Industrial

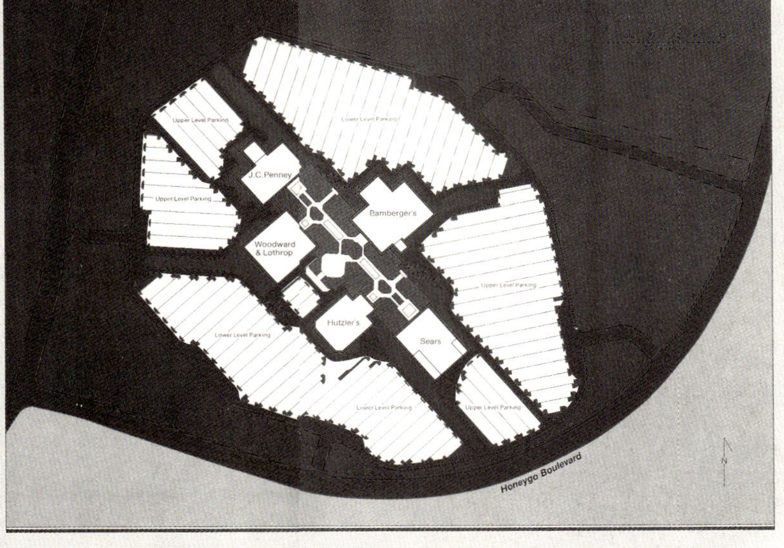

Client: The Rouse Co.
Design firm: RTKL Associates, Inc.,
Baltimore, Maryland
Designers: Phillips Engelke, Judy
Staples
Architect: RTKL Associates, Inc.;
Francis T. Taliaferro and Gary A.
Bowden, principals-in-charge; Paul F.
Jacob III, project architect
Fabricator: Belsinger Sign Co.

11.

Cambridge Center

A 24-acre site just across the river from Boston in the vicinity of MIT was cleared in the 1960s as part of the Federal Urban Renewal Program, but left undeveloped until recently. Now, an ambitious mixed-use complex, known as Cambridge Center, is underway, containing corporate, commercial and light industrial development. It promises new life for the somewhat down-at-heel Kendall Square area of Cambridge.

Asked to design a graphic identity for the Center and develop a comprehensive graphics plan, designers Herman and Lees decided that "high-tech" imagery would appropriately reflect the proximity to MIT and the technological sophistication of the Center's primary tenants. They describe the symbol they designed as "two concentric C's for Cambridge Center, scanned vertically to imply a high-tech image, and rendered into an almost tactile and three-dimensional form, expressive of mathematically-derived relationships and technological components." The symbol appears on site identification signing, a development opportunities manual, other printed matter aimed at attracting potential developers, construction workers' T-shirts, and numerous activities related to development and business in the Center.

In addition to the symbol design, Herman and Lees developed site signing for the Cambridge Redevelopment Authority, standards for traffic control signs, and designed and implemented building identification and commercial tenant signing and directories for the first buildings to be completed. Site identification signing consists of banner clusters announcing the main "gateways," and a large-scale kiosk with area map, site map and directory. Smaller-scale kiosks are placed at street corners and other strategic pedestrian circulation points.

The kiosks are internally illuminated and have light "slots" running up their sides to underscore their high-tech imagery. Signing for the first two buildings uses Helvetica Regular throughout, but in each case, materials are selected to complete the architecture. But while the hardware may differ in different buildings, a consistent directory insert system has been devised that can be employed in all buildings. Signing for commercial tenants emphasizes the use of fabric to reiterate the theme of the entry banners.

A spectrum of earth tones was chosen for the banners to complement the brick of the buildings. Kiosks and identifying signs are a warm shade of brown. Banners are nylon; kiosks fiberglass; and other graphics rendered in aluminum and brushed stainless steel to match architectural finishes. One recurring problem during the implementation of the designs was the fact that material colors in the field tended to be much lighter than the swatches from which they were chosen. In the end, the problem was solved by having large-scale fabric samples submitted for approval in the field before fabrication.

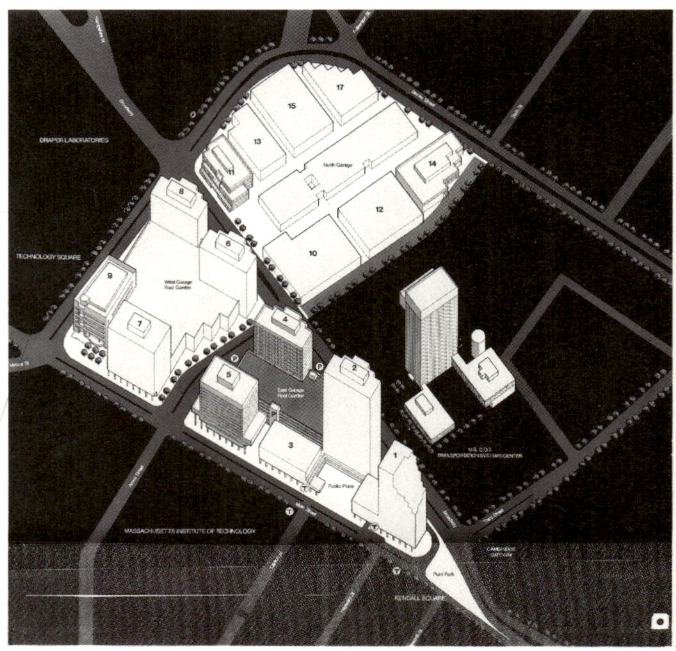

1.

2.

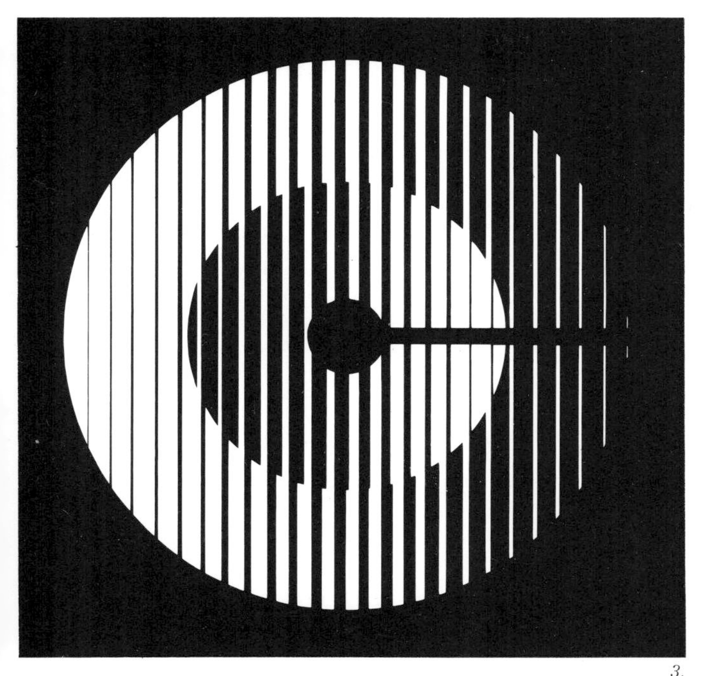

1, 2. Location and components of the Cambridge Center.
3, 4. High-tech imagery appears in symbol based on two concentric C's for Cambridge Center.
5. Early design study showing placement of banners.

3.

4.

5.

6.

7.

8.

9.

Client: Cambridge Redevelopment
Authority
Design firm: Herman and Lees
Associates, Cambridge, MA
Designers: John Lees, principal; John
Roll, Marla Schay, project designers;
Lonn Beaudry, Greg Wright, Sarah
Speare, staff designers
Planning consultants: Monacelli
Associates
Fabricators: Steel Art; Letterama
Consultants: Carol Johnson and
Associates, landscape architects; William
Lam Associates, lighting consultant;
Moshe Safdie and Associates, architects;
Boston Properties, developer

10.

11.

6. Building identification sign.
7. Prototype banner.
8. Illuminated site map.
9. Identity/information pylon.
10. Circular reception/information desk.
11. Studying the desk top directory.
12. Building identification sign.

12.

Mazza Gallerie

Turn-of-the-century Vienna and the precursors of modernism were the inspiration for an environmental design program aimed at making more inviting a five-year-old shopping mall, designed originally by the office of John Carl Warnecke. When Baltimore architects and designers RTKL were hired to make renovations, their mandate was to give this somewhat brutalist travertine-clad box a new sense of human scale and excitement that would attract attention in a high-fashion retail district and improve business. Studies of the building itself, and of the work of Viennese designers Josef Hoffman, Otto Wagner and Koloman Moser, led to the concept of an applied black-and-white tile motif to create pattern and visual excitement on the building exterior and around escalator columns and elevator entrances inside the Gallerie.

The entire pedestrian level of the building facade was wrapped in patterned tile; brass logo plaques situated next to each street entrance; and the travertine and dark-tinted glass around the main entry replaced by clear glass to yield entering views of the interior. A dramatic three-story interior space has thus been created which is bright with sunlight, plants and a specially designed and fabricated 13′ by 18′ tapestry.

Inside, the same tile pattern carries through to the elevator entrances and escalator columns. The atrium has been repainted and relit, and each level surrounded with a screened, etched glass design on the balustrades. Brass bands

1.

2.

1, 2. *Black-and-white tile theme, inspired by Viennese precursors of the Modern movement, humanize pedestrian aspect of a somewhat brutalist shopping mall.*
3. *Entry plaques are engraved brass.*
4. *Benguiat Medium and Futura Book were the typefaces used to give form and impact to the signing.*

3.

4.

have been added to existing railings; brass signs and directories introduced; and a turn-of-the-century Viennese café added as a new and elegant focus for the atrium.

It was thought at first that more expensive structural changes would be needed to achieve a sufficiently ameliorating result. But since these would have seriously disrupted business in the Mazza Gallerie, a more modest, cosmetic solution was sought. The black-and-white tile theme—stemming as it does from the transitional period between eclecticism, Art Nouveau and modernism—is appropriate in another transitional period in architecture and design. If it is no longer thought outrageous to add ornament to a modern building, RTKL nevertheless thought it important to find a vocabulary vested in the roots of the modern movement and not therefore antithetical to the building itself.

Client: 5300 Wisconsin Avenue Joint Venture; Prudential Insurance Co. of America (managing partner)
Design firm: RTKL Associates, Inc., Baltimore
Designers: Ann Dudrow, Jay Schwartz, Phillips Engelke, Judy Staples, Dan Snyder
Architect: RTKL Associates, Inc.; Ted A. Niederman, principal-in-charge; Kevin Dougherty, project architect; Paul Sweeney, project manager
Fabricator: Jack Stone Co.
Consultant: Bovini/Kondos Associates, Inc. (lighting)

Environmental Graphics/88

6.

7.

8.

9.

*Tapestry, 13' by 18', hangs just within the
entry.*
*Bold, illuminated site signing gives
character as well as direction.*
*Directories have sculptural as well as
informational impact.*
*Atrium space was repainted and relit, with
etched-glass designs on balustrades.*
*10. Brochure introducing the new Mazza
is a stylized interpretation of the black-and-
white grid theme inspired by turn-of-the-
century Vienna.*

10.

The Casebook jurors were unanimous in applauding the Minnesota Zoo's new signing and graphics program, partly because they were beguiled by the animal logo, numerals and directional arrow by which the major components of the zoo are identified. Most dramatic of these is the integration of the moose—an important state animal—into the letter "M" for Minnesota to become the zoo's symbol and logotype. The symbol has been translated into a monolithic concrete entrance sculpture, which even on the grand scale loses none of its appeal.

The five major exhibit areas or zoo trails are identified by numerals, each of which incorporates the image of an animal resident of that trail—for example, #1 (Ocean Trail) is a Beluga whale; #3 (Minnesota Trail) is a swimmer beaver; #5 (Northern Trail) is a camel. The directional arrow, called a guide bird, is a synthesis of an arrow and a bird in flight. It appears on interior and exterior pedestrian signs as well as on those for vehicular traffic.

The program was extensive—replacing a previous system (see Environmental Graphics Casebook 4, pages 17-20) but using the former sign structures wherever possible. This proved quite easy to do, as they were generally well placed and could be painted a charcoal brown to match architectural details, such as railings. The basic graphic color scheme is black-and-white against this charcoal background. Thus, although all signs are clear and easily legible, they are low key, allowing the animals and people to take center stage.

In addition to the zoo symbol and logotype and identifying symbols for the trails, the monorail and cross-country ski run, designer Lance Wyman developed a complete custom typeface to be used on all major signing, as well as a hand-out zoo leaflet explaining how the graphic symbols are derived and employed. The symbols and typography are cut and applied film (using a system of precision image cutting) which has the advantage of being both durable and easy for the zoo staff themselves to apply. Implementation of the graphics program is being carried out by Adele Smith and her graphic design staff at the zoo. The new graphics are applied to two types of existing sign structures—1′6″ by 9′ aluminum overhead signs and 1′6″ by 7′ pylons. A 2′8″ by 20′ entrance pylon is dominated by the moose logo.

Before any design concepts were developed, the designers conducted an on-site evaluation of the existing graphics and interviewed numerous members of the zoo community. This dialogue continued throughout the evolution and refinement of the program, which was constantly reviewed by zoo staff and zoo volunteers. This ensured that all problems surfaced and were dealt with, and exhibition areas that visitors somehow seemed to be passing by were much more clearly identified. The idea of using the moose as the zoo symbol came out of these conversations.

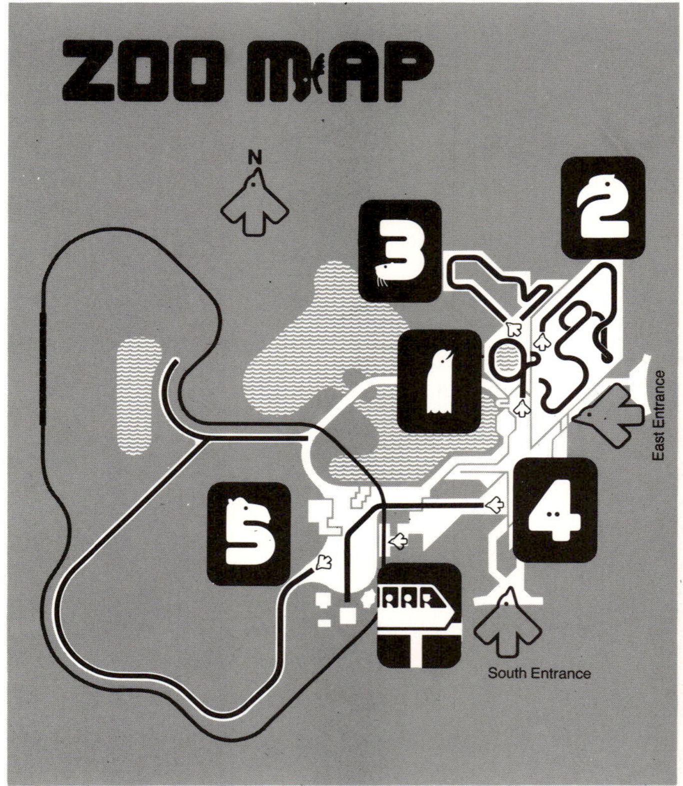

1. The Moose-M symbol for the zoo.
2-6. The five trail symbols each has an identifying numeral based on a major species to be found therein.
7. Zoo logo.
8, 9. Symbols appear again with great effect on zoo map, and on directional signs within the building. Directional "guide bird" arrow maintains this lighthearted touch.

3.    4.   5.    6.

9.

10.

11.

12.

13.

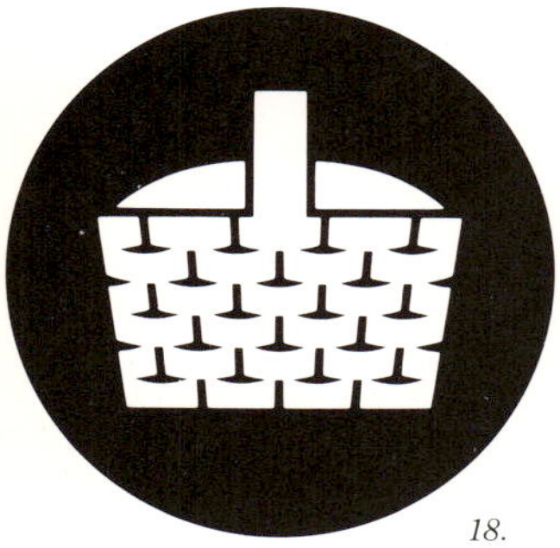

18.

19.

20.

21.

25.

26.

10-17. Variations of the "guide bird" arrow.
18-24. Witty but informative pictograms.
25. Moose logo translated into concrete to become dramatic entrance monolith.
26. Arrows and numerals appear on site pylons.

Environmental Graphics/92

14.

15.

16.

17.

22.

23.

24.

Client: Minnesota Zoological Gardens (Apple Valley, MN)
Design firm: Lance Wyman Ltd., New York City
Designers: Lance Wyman, Linda Iskander, Stephen Schlott
Architect: Interdesign, Inc.
Fabricator: Heritage Display (formerly Custom Display, Inc.)

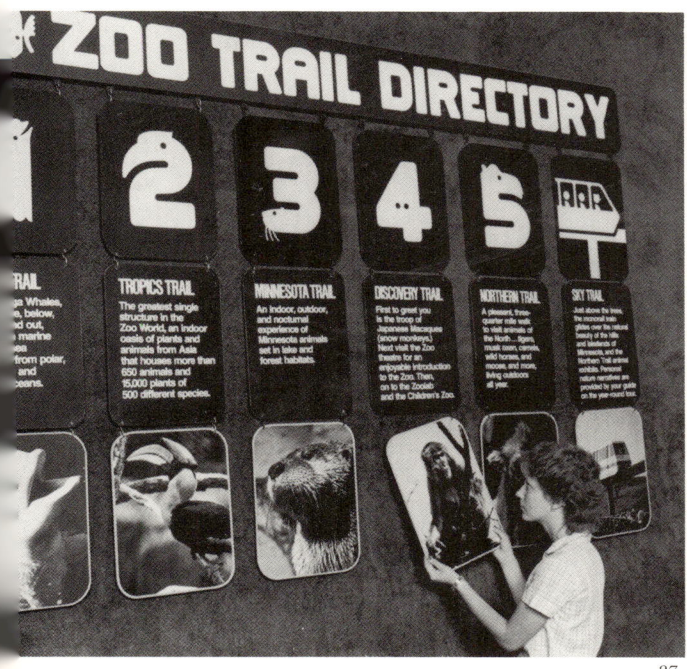

27.

28.

Directory combines symbols with photos of species and objects from which they were derived.
Designers evolved a complete custom typeface for the zoo.

Air Force Sign Standards

Casebook juries are always sympathetic to designers who cope well with a bureaucracy. Understanding the complex parameters and approval processes within which government contracts must be carried out, they are ready to applaud a solution that succeeds in being genuinely creative. Herman and Lees' Air Force Sign Standards Program was unanimously judged to fall within this category. The jury thought that, on both the visual and psychological levels, the new standards would have positive results. They would orient personnel and visitors within an enhanced esthetic environment, and at the same time help to promote a sense of optimism and personal commitment within a structured military framework.

Part of the Federal Design Improvement Program sponsored by the National Endowment for the Arts, the new standards program has a broad field of potential application—presently, 113 Air Force bases in the U.S. and 41 overseas. There is, of course, considerable architectural and topographical variety among these facilities, and one of the chief aims of the graphics program was to establish some kind of unity among them. In order to cope with a diversity of signing functions, the graphic standards were developed for five definable purposes: identification, direction, regulation, information, and motivation. This last category posed something of a challenge—how to devise a framework for traditional moral symbols, such as the old squadron emblems, within the

1.

1. Old signs were dull and confusing.
2. Page from manual detailing exterior community identification signs. Manual shows how local stations may implement the program themselves.
3. Cover and pages from the manual.
4, 5. New signs are clear, attractive and adaptable to different kinds of mounting.

ordered professionalism of the modern Air Force. Identification signs had to be divided into the strictly military, and those marking buildings such as the commissary or recreational facilities that would be used by the community as well—the latter group obviously needing an image a little freer, more colorful, more personal. Herman and Lees therefore developed a special community identification symbol and laid out a series of standards, different from, but within the general character of, those for the strictly military signs. For example, a different background color and a broader color palette were allowed, and the incorporation, where appropriate, of commerical logotypes was encouraged to add vitality.

After visiting several bases here and in England, and holding extensive interviews with military and civilian personnel, Herman and Lees not only developed the entire graphic standards program, and supervised its installation at three Air Force bases; they also compiled an extraordinarily detailed and comprehensive sign standards manual to enable staff at the individual bases to implement the program themselves. The manual details the graphic elements of the program and includes sign structure drawings and specifications, sign placement standards, and instructions on the preparation of a base master plan for signing. Although it includes all needed technical material, it is written for the layman to understand. It will also include a special appendix giving standards for

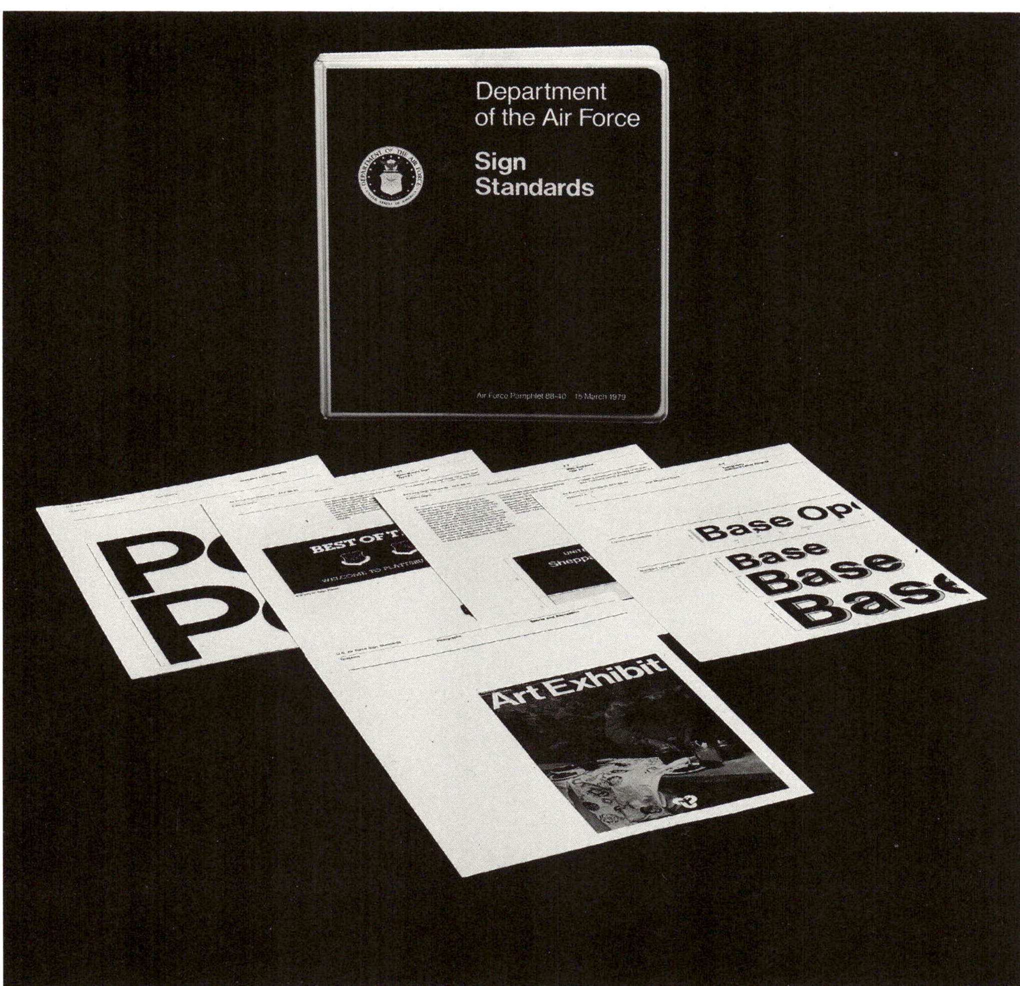

3.

4.

5.

bases whose buildings are of historical architectural significance.

With the anticipated breadth of application (and an implementation budget of $100,000 to $150,000 for each base) in mind, Herman and Lees were careful to specify materials, type styles and colors that meet all relevant federal standards and are easy to obtain. Colors of exterior signing, for example, conform to Federal Highway Administration standards; hardware is chiefly aluminum and steel; type is Helvetica.

6.

7.

8.

9.

Client: U.S. Air Force, Directorate of Engineering and Services; James Enloe, HQ USAF/LEEE, Bolling AFB, Washington, DC
Design firm: Herman and Lees Associates, Cambridge, MA.
Designers: John Lees, principal; Jon Roll, project designer; Stewart Monderer, Doug Davies, Greg Wright, staff designers
Architect: James Enloe (USAF), project officer
Fabricators: Spanjer Brothers; W.H. Brady Co.

6-9. Helvetica is used throughout. Signing hardware is chiefly aluminum and steel. Symbols and standards are devised and detailed to characterize sign categories— community, military, etc.